CHRISTIANITY AND PHILOSOPHY

Nihil Obstat

VINCENT L. KENNEDY, C.S.B.

Imprimatur

✠ JAMES C. McGUIGAN
Archiep. Torontinus

June 24th, 1939.

Christianity and Philosophy

ETIENNE GILSON

Professor in the Collège de France
Director of Studies, The Institute
of Mediaeval Studies, Toronto

Translated by
RALPH MacDONALD, C.S.B.

PUBLISHED FOR THE
INSTITUTE OF MEDIAEVAL STUDIES BY

Sheed & Ward
NEW YORK   LONDON
1939

Printed in the U. S. A.
for Sheed & Ward
New York and London

CONTENTS

PREFACE

THE last of the five chapters which compose this volume was written first and is the only one published to date. Originally it was a conference delivered to a Catholic audience at the invitation of Mr. François Veuillot. I have retained both subject and title just as they were proposed to me and as I had then accepted them. I do not think the chapters of which it has become the conclusion would have ever been written but that I received from my colleague Mr. M. Goguel and accepted another invitation, made in the name of a group of students in the Faculty of Protestant Theology of Paris, to speak to them of Christian philosophy. From this address, which is here read as Chapter One, the book was born. Yet, when I gave the address, I was far from thinking that I would write again on the subject. What I had said about it in *The Spirit of Mediaeval Philosophy* represented, and still represents in my mind the essentials of what I have to say concerning the notion of Christian philosophy. It turned out, however, to my great surprise, that by compelling myself to understand the attitude of reformed dogmatic theology on these questions, and seeing especially to what an involuntarily distorted image of Catholicism it was opposed, I became aware of certain tendencies, which had escaped me up to that time, and which, although doubtless they are not their cause, help nevertheless in understanding certain Catholic oppositions to the notion of Christian philosophy. I had therefore to push my inquiry far beyond what I had imagined, and in order to complete my discussion with a Calvinistic audience, to discuss opinions professed by some Catholic thinkers with whom I sincerely believed that all useful controversy was closed. It is my feeling of the importance of their object which has impelled me to publish these analyses, not in a spirit of controversy, for I know how futile controversy is, nor even to justify my own notion of Christian philosophy, which I willingly consider as open to discussion. The ultimate aim and purpose of the present book is to discuss certain conceptions of the relations of faith and reason which, were they to be accepted, would preclude the very possibility of the notion of a Christian philosophy by making it a contradiction in terms. Having tried elsewhere to establish the reality of Christian philosophy as an historically knowable fact, I am attempting here to discover, within the very essence of the Catholic faith, the roots of its theoretical possibility, or in other words, to establish that the notion of a Christian philosophy appears as consistent from the point of view of the Catholic truth taken in its entirety, and from no other one.

I am indebted to Mr. MacDonald, a student of the Institute of Mediaeval Studies, for having translated the French original of this book into English, thus providing me with an excellent opportunity to revise, correct, suppress, complete or clarify many passages of the French edition. The numerous differences that can be found between the two texts should therefore not be considered as resulting from liberties taken by the translator with the French original, but as expressing the more recent version, given by the author himself, of his own thought.

When I, a layman, was writing the following pages at the request of other laymen, I had to fight against the ever-recurring scruple that, with the best of intentions in the world, I was in fact trespassing upon theological ground. It was, therefore, a great joy for me to hear, not what I had said, but the very truth which I had laboured to express from the lips of a priest speaking with the theological authority of a priest. I feel deeply indebted to Father G. B. Phelan, President of the Institute of Mediaeval Studies, in Toronto, for permission to reprint his sermon as an introduction to this book. Its presence in that place does not signify that its theological truth is in any sense responsible for what I myself have said, but, on the contrary, to the full extent in which any one of my own statements might not agree with its theological truth, I myself disavow and withdraw that statement as contrary to the truth which it was my intention to express. My book is, therefore, in bondage to its Introduction, but its Introduction is by no means in bondage to my book. I am now satisfied that my readers will have heard, at least once, the truth to which I subscribe. For having so charitably set my conscience at rest, I beg to extend to Father Phelan the expression of my utmost gratitude.

ETIENNE GILSON

The Institute of Mediaeval Studies (Toronto)
December 14th, 1938

INTRODUCTION

Being a sermon preached by
The Reverend Father Gerald B. Phelan
President of the Institute of Mediaeval Studies
to the members of
The Catholic Educational Press Congress
held at
Marquette University, Milwaukee, Wisconsin,
October 14, 15, and 16, 1938.

IN LUMINE TUO VIDEBIMUS LUMEN.

Psalm 35, verse 10.

When God made man He made him out of the slime of the earth. Then, He breathed into his face the breath of life and man became a living soul. God made many animals before He made man and He gave them the power to increase and multiply, to reproduce their kind; He gave them eyes and ears and other senses to perceive all the things with which they were surrounded; and He also gave them a sort of natural skill in knowing what was good for them and what was harmful to them. We call this skill, "instinct". But He gave to none of the lower animals what He gave to man, namely, a mind to know what is true and a will to love what is good. Because man has a mind, or reason, and a will he is far greater than all the lower animals and, as the Psalmist says, just "a little less than the angels".

Because man has a rational soul he is made to the image and likeness of God. The perfect Image of God is the Son of God, the Second Person of the Most Holy Trinity. Being creatures, we cannot be *perfectly* like God, as His Only Begotten Son is. But we were truly created in His image and likeness and so we are as like God as it is possible for us creatures to be. For, as the Bible says, "The light of Thy countenance is sealed upon us, O Lord!"

The reason why men are such noble creatures is precisely because they have a mind or reason. Such is their nature. And, the more they develop their mind as it should be developed, the better will they know what is true and love what is good and the more they will become like God who knows all truth and is all good.

God wanted His noblest earthly creature, man, to know and love Him even better than he could by the natural powers of his soul. He therefore gave man an extra-special gift, called grace. By that gift man was raised so high above his natural powers that he was able to know God and to love Him as God knows and loves Himself, although, of course, not so perfectly. Thus, by the gift of grace man was able to live like God, Whose life consists in eternally knowing and loving Himself, besides being able to live like the creature that he was; for, grace is the principle of supernatural life just as the soul is the principle of natural life.

But God also wanted man to show his appreciation for these wonderful gifts of nature and of grace and to acknowledge that they all came from God, the Giver of all good gifts. So, He told man that he must manifest his obedience to his Creator by refraining from eating the forbidden fruit. Now, God did not want man to obey Him just for the sake of mak-

ing him obey, as bullies do to smaller boys just for the satisfaction of showing how big and strong they are. No! God
is kind and good. He never acts like a tyrant or a bully.
He loved man so much that He had given him many great
gifts of nature and, to crown them all, He gave him a share
in His very own divine Life. He only wanted man to love
Him in return. The only reason, therefore, why God wished
man to obey Him and to abide by His commands was because that is the only way man can show his love for God.
For, love is manifested in giving. When we love somebody
dearly we wish to make gifts to him. But the only gift that
man can make to God is the gift of his will, his heart, his
love because that is the only thing which man possesses as his
very own, the only thing he can refuse to God, since all the
rest of his possessions, including his very life, belong to God
already.

But, man refused to give to God the gift of his heart
and will. He disobeyed God and ate the forbidden fruit.
He yielded to the temptation of the devil, who promised him
great rewards, particularly for his intelligence, saying that if
he disobeyed God and ate the forbidden fruit he would be
like God, knowing good and evil. So, through a sinful desire to penetrate the secret of God, the mystery of good and
evil, by his own unaided efforts—by pride of intellect, in
other words—man disobeyed God and fell from His favour
and grace. The sin of eating "the fruit of that forbidden
tree whose mortal taste brought death into the world and all
our woe" was a sin of intellectual pride and thus was man's
mind, his reason, contaminated by sin. If ever he were to
return to the grace and love of God, and be turned away from
the deceits and falsehoods of the devil, his mind must once

more be made holy and humble and he must pay homage of his understanding to the truth of God.   In other words, he must sanctify his intelligence.

God did not leave man in the hopeless and miserable plight into which the sin he committed had plunged him but, in His great mercy, He promised a Redeemer who would restore man to divine favour and give him back the gifts of grace he had wantonly cast away.   So, in due course of time, He sent His Only Begotten Son, the Splendour of the Father, the Light that enlighteneth every man that cometh into the world, to rescue man from the power of darkness and lead him back into the light and truth of God.

Nevertheless, man still bears the scars of that original defeat at the hands of Satan.   Because of the sin of our first parent we are doomed to live with our understanding darkened, our will weakened and our whole nature strongly inclined to evil.   Yet, by God's grace, we can overcome those disadvantages and heal those wounds; but the only way is to live in the Light of the Word made Flesh.   He will gladly enlighten and sanctify our minds, soften the hardness of our hearts and strengthen us against temptation if only we do not refuse His Light and grace.   For, Jesus Christ, God's Only Begotten Son, was born of the Virgin Mary, suffered under Pontius Pilate, and being crucified, died and was buried and rose again from the dead, all, to save us from the penalty of sin.   He is the Light which enlighteneth every man that cometh into the world.   He is the true Light.   He is the only Light; there is no other.

Unless the Light of the Word of God made Flesh shine upon our minds, seeing, we shall not understand.   And, whosoever shuts his soul against the shining of that Light must sit in the darkness and the shadow of death; though the Light shine in that darkness, the darkness cannot comprehend it. But, whosoever opens his soul to the shining of that Light shall see His glory, the glory, as it were, of the Only-Begotten of the Father, full of grace and truth. The light of the Eternal Word shone in the beginning, for in the beginning was the Word and the Word was with God and the Word was God; it shone, too, in the moment of creation upon the works of His hands and He saw that all things were good, for all things were made in Him who is the Light and without Him was made nothing that was made; it shone, too, and especially, upon God's noblest creature on earth, man, to give him being, life and grace and to make him unto the image and likeness of God; at length, in the fullness of time, the eternal Light which is the Word came into this world to be the Light of men and was born, not of blood nor of the will of the flesh nor of the will of man but of God. And the Word was made Flesh and dwelt amongst us . . . full of grace and truth.

The Word of God still dwells amongst us, for of His fullness we have all received. By grace we truly live the life of the Emmanuel, the God with us, and that is why the life which is in Him is the Light of men. *In ipso vita erat et vita erat lux hominis.* By that Light our minds are made holy; in that Light our intelligence is sanctified.

The truly Catholic mind is thus a holy mind, a sanctified intelligence; and it is as necessary to have and as difficult to acquire as holiness itself. It is necessary because unless our minds are made holy we cannot truly understand ourselves, the world or God. Nothing on earth is any longer the same since Christ redeemed the world. Nothing is truly intelligible, nothing has meaning or significance except through Him, with Him and in Him—*per Ipsum, cum Ipso et in Ipso*. The Mystery of the Incarnation has changed the face of the earth and whosoever would understand the life of man (his personal life as well as his social and political rights and duties) must view it the light of that great mystery. Thus, is the sanctification of the intelligence a necessary thing. It is difficult to acquire because it entails the constant practice of virtue, especially the virtue of humility —the humility of mind. The power of reason is, we are well aware, the true source of our dignity as men and we are all prone to put our trust in it. It is, indeed, true that by giving us reason and intelligence God has made us only a little less than the angels and we are loath to humble that intelligence even before the Light and Truth of God. But human reason, great as it is in comparison to the limited powers of the lower animals, is only as a flickering candle-light in comparison to the brightness of Eternal Light. We find it very difficult to realize this profound truth; so, constant effort, self-denial, vigilance and self-criticism are necessary to keep our minds in permanent and humble submission to the Word who was in the Beginning with God. Thus, is the sanctification of the intelligence most difficult to acquire.

The Word of God is, in very truth, the Light which enlighteneth *every* man that cometh into the world and of His fullness we have *all* received. But some of those who have received of His fullness are called to bear witness to the Light, as did the man who was sent from God and whose name was John. Catholic writers, speakers and journalists are among that number. And, if they would give testimony of the Light, that all men might believe in Him, as John the Baptist did, then must they aim at all times to see things in the light of that Eternal Truth. They must learn to think, to judge, to reason and to understand, not merely by the light of natural reason but under the guidance of the Light who is the life of men. They cannot truly place their intelligence at the service of God unless they strive to purify it of all worldliness and learn to look at every problem in the light of God and for the love of truth. In a word they must sanctify their intelligence.

It has always been and will ever be a difficult task to purify our minds of all that is of the earth, earthy, but in these modern days the work of sanctifying the mind is particularly hard. For the age in which we live has seen, on the one hand, the complete denial of the doctrine of original sin and, on the other hand, the grossest exaggerations of the teaching on the corruption of man's nature as a consequence of sin. The naturalism of Jean Jacques Rousseau and the heresy of Martin Luther have left their mark upon our generation. Against the one we must emphatically affirm the weakness of our nature, wounded by sin. Against the other we must strenuously deny that our nature was totally corrupted by the sin of our first parent.

We cannot either live or think as if sin had never laid its devastating finger on our souls; neither can we live or think as if sin has so far corrupted us that, even by the grace of God, we can do nothing good. Both the Rousseauistic *innocence of nature* and the Lutheran *corruption of nature* are false and unchristian doctrines. It is not true that the human mind may see and know the truth as clearly and as limpidly as though it had never been darkened by that first prevarication. Neither is it true that our intelligence is so blinded, as a result of original sin, that it can know nothing at all about God and His divine plans. It is true that sin has wounded us; that, as a consequence of sin our natural power of knowing and loving what is true and good has been weakened but our natural powers are still intact and, by the grace of God, they can be healed. So, while we stand firm in defense of that which constitutes our human dignity, while we strive to vindicate the value of God's precious gift of reason, we must also acknowledge the inherent weakness of human intelligence (are we not the lowest in the scale of intelligent beings?), a weakness increased as a consequence of sin—original sin, first of all and actual sin, as well. This acknowledgment will include the recognition of God's power to enlighten our minds, the humble submission of our reason to the Word who is the Light, the homage of our understanding to the God of all Truth and a prayer that He may send forth His Light that we may be re-created.

It is most important, therefore, for those who dedicate their intelligence to the service of Christ, as all good Catholic writers, journalists and speakers do, to understand and appreciate the difficulty of their task. For, they must use their *natural* talents in the service of *divine* Truth and it is no facile thing to keep one's equilibrium upon that narrow crest where Faith and reason meet, and balance to a nicety the respective rôles of nature and of grace in the practical issues of life. It is a still more difficult thing in these days when the whole tone of the civilization in which we live is not only thoroughly unchristian, but for a large part hostile to Christian thought and culture and, as Our Holy Father the Pope has said, fast lapsing into a condition worse than paganism. We are tempted to use in the service of God the

impure methods, the questionable tactics commonly and efficaciously used in the journalistic world where a passing vic-
tory over a rival paper or a sensational account of the news
of the day is regarded as more important than a statement
of what is true. This difficulty is increased still further by
the fact that Christian Charity demands that we refrain
from engaging in offensive personalities, disputes and
quarrels with our neighbours, even over the most important
issues in life but that we rather endeavour to lead our erring
brethren by gentler and more Christian means, even when
they maliciously attack us, to the light and knowledge of the
Word of God made Flesh. We must, indeed, always state
and expound God's holy truth uncompromisingly and we
must defend it with all zeal and vigour, fearlessly and without favour, but at the same time the love of our erring
neighbour must never be lessened by our hatred for his
error.

Let me therefore suggest some thoughts for your
prayerful reflection and meditation, thoughts which I sincerely hope may clarify the task of those who have chosen
to work out their salvation by devoting to Christ the service
of their intelligence through the medium of the written or
the spoken word.

It is essential, first of all, to remember that God does
not need our help in order to make His truth triumphant
over error. He is the God of Truth, the God of Power
and the God of Love. He knows the secrets of all hearts
and, if He so willed, could draw all men to Himself simply
by the inward whisperings of His grace. In the past He has,
on many occasions, suddenly enlightened the minds and
touched the hearts of men who prided themselves in the

power of their natural intelligence and He has brought them to their knees in grateful and enthusiastic acknowledgment of His infinite Truth and Love. To-day He still works miracles of grace without the help of men and sometimes even in spite of our awkward, though well-meaning, efforts. He could do likewise, if such were His holy Will, for all those whom we hope, by our tongues or pens, to bring to the knowledge of the truth. *Servi inutiles sumus;* God does not need us. It is well, I say, to keep this thought in mind so that when, by some blessed chance our words may bring the light of truth to some receptive mind, we may be prepared to say with all the sincerity of our hearts: *Non nobis, Domine, non nobis, sed nomini Tuo da gloriam!* Give not the glory to us, O Lord, but to Thy holy name!

In the second place I would remind you that, if it be true—as indeed it is—that God does not need even our best efforts in order to accomplish His holy purpose among men, it is still more true that He does not need our less worthy designs of pure worldly wisdom. There is no place in Catholic journalism or Catholic apologetics for any kind of petty human devices resorted to in order to dodge difficulties or to avoid facing issues squarely; there is no place for unfair half-truths which we may imagine will sometimes serve what is just and good but which, in reality, only support our personal opinions and antagonize honest people; there is no place for distorted interpretations of facts, one-sided accounts of complicated events, manipulation of evidence or suppression of facts we find hard to understand or to explain. It has been well, though vigorously, said that God does not need our lies. Truth is too sacred a thing to be tampered with like that. Radical sincerity in the search for truth, intellectual honesty in stating it when found, candour in acknowledging when we have made mistakes, and a deep reverence at all times for even the smallest item of truth—these are the characteristics of the Catholic mind which make it not unworthy of service in the cause of God's holy truth.

All this requires a sincere and honest love of truth as well as a profound respect for its sacred character. A love of truth for itself—the untouchable truth which we may learn but which we may not alter under penalty of betraying it—that is, indeed, a noble thing, yet it is an excellence open to man's natural capacity. Truth may be loved by reason for its natural fitness and its natural attractiveness. But reverence for the sanctity of truth can only come, in full measure at least, through those graces and gifts with which it has pleased God to adorn our natural intelligence, the gifts of Faith, Understanding, Knowledge and Wisdom—the theological Virtues and the Gifts of the Holy Ghost. For truth is not only true; it is also and above all holy. Therefore our intelligence must be made holy to deal with it. *Sancta sancte!*

In the third place, I should like to suggest for your reflection the consoling thought that, though God does not need our service or our help, He nevertheless has deigned to honour us in using the very talents He Himself has bestowed upon us, as instruments in the accomplishment of His divine purpose among men. We are the tools He chooses to employ in applying the fruits of His Redemption to the souls of men. Poor tools, no doubt, for such a sublime work, but they are mighty when God uses them.

But God will not use us against our will or without our

consent. We are privileged to coöperate with Him in the work of bringing the knowledge of His truth and love to men but He has left us free either to grant Him our meagre coöperation or to refuse it. All men are called by God to lend their assistance to His cause, but not all men respond. He has even left us free to choose, within the limits of our capacities, how we shall coöperate with Him in achieving His all-wise designs. All men are asked to devote their talents to His service; but all men have not the same talents and therefore cannot serve Him in the same way. One may serve Him as a labourer, another as a clerk, a third as a professional man and still another as a man of business, an executive, a manufacturer or in any other line of human endeavour. Only some, and you are among that number, are called to serve Him by their talents as writer, journalist, orator or teacher. Those who do so serve have freely consented to undertake this special work and have freely chosen to offer to God the homage of their intelligence. And, for such as these, the sanctification of the intelligence is of imperative and paramount importance. For, it is principally their intelligence which they offer to God as an instrument for the accomplishment of His holy will. Since, therefore, it were most unworthy to offer God a tainted gift, it behooves all who engage in these professions to make the instrument they offer to God as perfect an instrument as they can make it. They should give to God a mind which, on the one hand, is properly equipped for His holy service in so far as it is naturally capable of that perfection and, on the other hand, has been purified and made holy by the study and contemplation of Divine Truth.

To put this more concretely, let me say that those who have chosen to serve God by editing papers, writing books or articles, speaking in public or otherwise teaching or defending truth under any form, should bend their best efforts to the achievement of two distinct objects or purposes: first, to learn and master their trade and its technique; second, to learn and know the science of divine truth and know it well.

Every science and art has its own specific character. Journalism, writing, oratory, each has its own methods and its own technique; each has its own proper end and object; each can be pursued and practiced for its own sake, without regard to any possible use it may have in the service of religion. In other words, there is a right way and a wrong way of editing a paper or writing a story, whether the paper or the story is a good paper or a good story or the contrary. A bad paper can be well edited. A bad story can be well written. Consequently a man who has no religion at all and no concern for religion, no interest in it, may be a good journalist or a good writer, because journalism and literary production have their own proper techniques and standards of artistic value irrespective of the content of the articles or stories produced. Moveover, it is not only possible but, unfortunately, it happens all too frequently that Catholics who are journalists, writers and orators are not always Catholic journalists, Catholic writers and Catholic orators.

If, however, one wants to be a Catholic journalist, writer or orator, the first and most necessary thing is to be a good journalist, a good writer, a good orator, i.e., to master the highly specialized methods and techniques required for expert competence in these fields. In other words, one must know his job and be as expert in his calling as he can be before he can becomingly turn his talent to the defense and propagation of the truth. Poor science, poor philosophy, poor journalism, poor writing can never be good apologetics no matter how piously they may be used in defense of the Faith. The only way to make science, philosophy, or art of any kind good apologetics is to make them good science, good philosophy and good art. Piety cannot replace technique.

Finally, none can hope to be a good apologist, to serve God by the defense and propagation of His truth, if he does not know the doctrines he is expounding and the truth he is defending. A thorough knowledge of Christian doctrine is essential for a Catholic writer or journalist. A thorough knowledge, I say; not a merely sufficient knowledge adequate for one not engaged, as every Catholic journalist is, in publicly explaining and interpreting to others the Revealed Word of God, in combatting false opinions and erroneous views, in pointing the lessons of history and, in general, interpreting literature, art, current events and life as a whole in the light of the teachings of Christ. Where will the journalist, the writer, acquire such a knowledge of Christian doctrine except by studying theology, the Science of Divine Truth?

There is no valid reason on earth why laymen and laywomen should not study theology. There is no reason which should prevent them even from becoming experts in theology if they have the competence to do so, the opportunity and the means of pursuing that study with due seriousness and adequate direction. It is a mistake to imagine that theology is a sort of esoteric science, reserved exclusively to the clergy. Priests, it is true, must learn theology in order to discharge the duties of their sacred ministry. In like manner, lawyers must learn the law in order to perform the duties of their calling. There is nothing, however, to prevent a layman from also learning that divine science and even becoming more expert in theology than the majority of priests just as there is nothing to prevent a priest from studying the law and becoming more expert, more learned in the law, than the majority of lawyers. In point of fact, there are not a few laymen in the world to-day who are far better versed in theology than many priests, just as there are not a few priests who know more about the science of the law than many lawyers do. For those, however, be they laymen or priests, who undertake to do the work of a Catholic journalist or writer, a good knowledge of theology is essential. They *must* know theology, else their work will not be truly fruitful. Without training in theology, they would be most apt to make egregious errors regarding the precise teachings of Christ and His Holy Church and, in all good faith, defend and uphold what is in reality contrary to the truth. Such mistakes are not unknown in the columns of our Catholic papers and in many cases they are mainly due to a lack of theological accuracy. A journalist or writer who, on the contrary, has devoted time and study to the science of theology will know whereof he speaks and his words will bear weight with his readers and bring light and conviction to their minds.

Contact with Divine Truth both in study and in prayer will make the mind holy. The journalist or writer who gives himself up to the pursuit of that truth both through the intricate paths of theological science and in the silence and recollection of mental prayer will be enabled to use in a thoroughly enlightened way the natural power of his reason, the talent he has developed in the practice of his profession, the zeal and charity infused into his heart by God and turn them all to good advantage in bringing to others a knowledge and a love of the Truth that was in the beginning with God, that in his light they may see light. *In lumine Tuo videbimus lumen.*

May God bless your efforts, my dear friends, and bring to you light and strength, courage and perseverance in your efforts to serve Him faithfully by tongue and pen. May He sanctify your minds, prosper your art and fill your hearts with the love of Him who for love of you and all of us sent His Only Begotten Son to rescue us from the darkness which sin had cast upon our souls and to lead us into the Light and Truth of God. May He give power to your voice and pen that you may bear witness to the truth as did the man who was sent from God and whose name was John, that through your efforts, as through his, all men may believe in the Word who was in the Beginning and who was made Flesh and dwelt amongst us.

Amen.

Reprinted from The Proceedings of the Catholic Educational Press Congress, October 1938. Marquette University Press, Milwaukee, Wisconsin.

I

NATURE AND PHILOSOPHY

PERMIT me first of all to express my appreciation of the signal mark of confidence bestowed on me in being asked to address you, and allow me at the same time to excuse myself for having made a slight change, not in the subject you proposed to me, but in the title: *Christian Philosophy*. As a matter of fact it seemed to me that it would be of profit to all of us, and to myself in the first place, to carry the discussion to an even deeper level. I intend, therefore, to speak to you this evening on the fundamental problem of the relations between Christianity and philosophy. Before taking up the question itself, however, I think I should make clear to you how I intend to treat it.

To attempt to determine dogmatically what ought to be, in one and the same conscience, the relations of Christianity to philosophy would seem, at first sight, to be the most natural method. I shall not, however, follow that method, precisely because it is natural, whereas here we are faced by a problem which surpasses the order of nature. However different may be our religious convictions, we are certainly agreed in admitting that, once Christianity is involved in a problem, it no longer depends uniquely, nor even principally, on us to discover the solution. We may even say that, should one of us have the good fortune to find the solution, and also the art required to formulate it in universally understandable terms, *he* could not be the sole cause of his hearer's accepting it, nor *they*, that it be accepted by them.   More than that, his own acceptance of it would not depend on himself alone: *non ego autem, sed gratia Dei mecum.*[1]   Let us beg God, therefore, to enlighten us, that His grace accomplish its work in us, for it alone can reveal the truth to us, and once revealed make us embrace it.

In a dialogue of this kind, the rôle of the human interlocutor is necessarily modest, yet not completely vain. Indeed it may even be of real importance when the inquirer is a philosopher.   For, it seems to me, one of the essential tasks of a philosopher is to define what I might call "pure positions".   As a matter of fact, it is scarcely possible to encounter such positions concretely actualized, since men rarely seek them, and if they do find them, still more rarely do they abide by them.   Our natural tendency is to live comfortably in the impure region of compromise, whilst admitting principles which, if strictly applied, would preclude the facilities that compromise concedes.   Determining what a pure position would be is, of course, not the same thing as adopting it, but it is a beginning.   For, from the moment we see it, we at least know how we should have to think in order to render our manner of life justifiable, or alternatively how we should have to live in order to reconcile ourselves with our manner of thinking.

One way of solving the problem without getting implicated in an illegitimate compromise, would be to refuse to the Christian, as such, all right to philosophical knowledge. It is a long time ago since some ecclesiastical writers thought of that solution.   From the very first centuries of the Church two great spiritual families began to differentiate, and they will doubtless ever live side by side within it: the family of the friends of philosophy and the family of its enemies. Tatian might be chosen as the prototype of the second group, and the unknown author of the *Irrisio philosophorum* might readily be his second. Lest we lose ourselves in history, however, let us recall simply that the twelfth century, which witnessed the rise of logical studies, rang with the protests of many theologians against the use of profane sciences. For St. Peter Damiani, for example, there was none of them, not even grammar, which might not prove dangerous. In his opinion, the devil was the first professor of grammar. And see what he did with it! By telling our first parents: *Eritis sicut Dii,* he taught them to decline *Deus* in the plural. The first lesson in grammar was at the same time a lesson in polytheism. What, then, shall we say of logic? What harm will it not cause in theology if it is allowed to get in there? Remember that miracles and mysteries are not reducible to syllogisms and that God cannot be submitted to the principle of contradiction. Let the Christian, therefore, leave this pagan science to the Pagans. It has value only for a pagan world. When God wished to save the world, He did not choose twelve professors of philosophy and make them His apostles. No, He chose humble, simple, ignorant men. They are and ought to remain our masters, for they are the bearers of the Word of Christ and it is His word alone that saves: *In Deo igitur, qui vera est sapientia, quaerendi et intelligendi finem constitue.*[2]

This "holy simplicity", which Hus was later to meet on a tragic occasion, found in the Middle Ages numerous supporters and relentless defenders. Nevertheless it still remains to be seen whether the purity of their position, not indeed of their intentions, was of a nature to justify their zeal. The sentiment which animated them is quite evident, for they themselves never tired of expressing it. Christians, priests and monks, these men pass judgment in the light of one sole and unique concern, that, namely, of salvation. If one wished to play a mean joke on them by defining their position in a formal syllogism, one might almost say this: Salvation is the only thing that matters; but the word of God is salvation; therefore the word of God is all that matters. This is the essential and persistent conviction underlying the doctrines of all the anti-philosophers throughout the whole history of the Church. Whether they say it with blunt rudeness, as St. Peter Damiani, or with a more dignified and measured reserve, as St. Bernard, or with the anguish of a troubled conscience, as did Otloh of Saint Emmeram in the *Book of his temptations*, all mean fundamentally the same thing. A Christian must renounce the world in order to save himself. A monk embraces the religious life solely for the purpose of realizing the Christian life in its perfect form; the monk must therefore leave the world completely, and since philosophy is of the world, the monk must have nothing whatever to do with it. *Conversus a saecularibus* and *conversus a philosophia* are for him one and the same thing. Why then should he engage in researches, which are not only useless but dangerous for one who is pursuing the one thing necessary: salvation? One does not light a candle, says Peter Damiani, in order to see the sun.

That state of mind, so widespread in the Middle Ages, still reveals itself today, though somewhat less harshly, to every reader of the *Imitation of Christ*.[3] It is hardly necessary to add that each of us feels within himself that which lends to this attitude a lasting value, a character of near inevitability. The masters of the *contemptus saeculi* were right in this sense at least, that as preachers and moralists, their zeal for conversion could not be more forcefully expressed. Who, then, could blame them for having put in the strongest possible words that of which they wished to convince us for the salvation of our soul? In this sense, and so they meant it, not only should philosophy be eliminated, but even dogmatic theology ought to be relegated to a secondary place: "I would rather feel compunction than know its definition" [4]. Nothing is truer. Nevertheless their position admits of a difficulty, which they chose to ignore, although their adversaries never left off placing it before their eyes. Was not this philosophy, with which they would have nothing to do, the work of reason? But natural reason itself is the work of God; it is even in us as a divine image, the mark left by the Creator on His work. Of it the Scriptures say: *"The light of thy countenance, O Lord, is signed upon us."* [5] We are called upon to despise the image of God in us: but that would be to despise God Himself in us! Without doubt that is why St. Augustine recommended the study of dialectics as necessary to the Christian,[6] though no one would suspect him of granting an excessive self-sufficiency to nature. Again it was these same reasons which impelled Berengarius of Tours, in his tract *De sacra coena*, to justify the use of logic in matters of theology. We know that because of it he finally denied transubstantiation and no one would affect surprise at the violent attacks that were then directed against his conclusions. But that is not the question. The only point with which we are here concerned is whether or not he was right in considering the use of logical reasoning legitimate in theology. More precisely it is a question of knowing what Catholic theologians could validly reply when he said to them: "It is a noble heart that has recourse in everything to dialectics, for to have recourse to it is to have recourse to reason; but he who has not recourse to it, is nevertheless made to the image of God by his reason; it is, therefore, his very honour that he despises, and he cannot renew himself from day to day in the image of God." What is the reply to that? What can a Catholic dispute in it? That man is made to the image of God; that the image of God in man is reason; that it is an honour from which we are bound to derive every possible benefit, all that is unshakeably true even from the point of view of Augustine, of Peter Damiani, or of Bernard of Clairvaux. But once reason is accepted logic will have to be accepted as well, and what will then become of all the denunciations of the philosophers and of the condemnation which has oppressed them? Theologically, as well as philosophically, the position of the anti-dialecticians of the Middle Ages was as precarious as their zeal was firm. No wonder then if in spite of their religious ardour, of their authority, sometimes even of their sanctity, the movement favouring the profane studies grew continuously in the course of the Middle Ages. Philosophy, the handmaid of theology, became more and more indispensable to its mistress, until finally theology could be studied only after a lengthy preparatory course in philosophy. Even today anyone unacquainted with Aristotle will understand very little in the *Summa* of St. Thomas Aquinas.

What had been with Catholic writers but the vehement expression of their personal aversion to philosophy was to become, at the time of the Reformation, something essentially different: a condemnation of philosophy fully conscious of its theological implications. For Luther started out essentially as a monk haunted by the need of salvation, heartily despising everything that was of no use for it. It is well known how unrelentingly he expressed himself concerning the intrusion of dialectics, dialecticians and philosophical reasoning in general into the realms of theology. If he had done only that, his attitude would have had nothing original in it, not even its coarseness and violence, in which regard some mediaevalists perhaps even outdid him. True enough, he qualifies all commentary on the physics of Aristotle as "rhetorical declamation on filth"; for him philosophy is folly, and the theology which uses it is only badly boiled grounds; *Ve tibi maledicta blasphemia, ut incocta est haec fex philosophiae!* All that is certainly not very amiable; but Saint Peter Damiani did not scruple to treat the profane sciences as "prostitutes of the theatre", which wasn't any more amiable, and even, with a quite biblical sharpness, to accuse their followers of confusing the honest daughters of Laban with the "lupanar concubines".[7] What was new in the Reformation, on this point at least, was neither the tone, nor even the sentimental attitude, but the doctrine. For the first time in the history of Christianity, this radical condemnation, levelled at philosophy by so many Christians, eloquently formulated but never turned into a theological doctrine, was at last seeking its theoretical justification.

We shall better understand the real novelty in Luther's attitude by comparing it with that of St. Augustine to whom he often referred. *Augustinus meus totus est,* said he in his *De servo arbitrio.*[8] That he should have lived in this illusion is, in one sense, not beyond comprehension. It was to be expected that the Doctor of grace should hold the attention of a man for whom grace had become the whole of the religious life, and religious life itself the only life that matters. There is, nevertheless, an irreconcilable cleavage between the attitude of Luther and that of St. Augustine.

Nowhere in the writings of the Bishop of Hippo will be found the radical condemnation of fallen nature which constantly flows from the pen of Luther. Quite to the contrary, fallen nature remains in his eyes so beautiful, so good and so great, that he did not hesitate to say that had God created it such as it is after the fall, it would still suffice to prove the infinite wisdom of its Author. This theme, which I have elsewhere proposed to call the "eulogy of fallen nature", seems to me to express admirably an essential aspect of authentic Augustinianism, that, namely, of St. Augustine himself. It is unfolded at length in an important text of the *City of God*, where the author enumerates "the goods that God has conferred on nature, even vitiated and damned (*quae ipsi quoque vitiatae damnataeque naturae contulit*), or that He still confers on it now". If all Chapter 24 of the XXII book is reread attentively, it will be seen how completely a stranger St. Augustine remained to what was to be the very heart of Lutheran theology. For him "God has not taken from the condemned all that He gave him, since then he would no longer exist at all", and let us not imagine that what God has left him is something insignificant; "It is He Who has given understanding to the human soul . . . And, though sometimes sterile, this capacity which reasoning nature, coming from the divine hands, has for so many goods, what a good it is in itself, what an admirable masterpiece of the All-powerful! Who will be capable of expressing or even conceiving it fittingly? In fact, even leaving aside those arts of living well and of attaining to the immortal bliss called the virtues, which the grace of God alone, which is in Christ, gives to the children of promise and of the kingdom, has not the human mind discovered and put into practice, whether for our needs or for our pleasure, so many arts, and so great, where the power of thought and of reason is revealed so excellent even in the pursuit of superfluous, dangerous or even pernicious things, that it attests what a great good this nature is in itself, which has been able to discover, learn or practice these arts? . . . What a prodigious variety of signs, and in the first place, words and letters invented to communicate and persuade our thoughts? . . . What seductions have poetry, music, the voice, worked out to charm the ear? With what wisdom have the sciences of number and extension discovered the situation and course of the celestial bodies? Briefly with what an infinity of natural knowledge is not the human intelligence filled? Who could describe it, especially if, instead of taking them in a group we wished to consider each separately? And in the defence even of errors and fallacies, who can appreciate with what splendour shone the minds of philosophers and heretics? For we speak here of the nature of human thought, the ornament of this mortal life, not of faith, and of the path of truth which leads to the immortal."[9] True, all these splendours, and many others which he emumerates, are for Augustine only consolations of the miserable and condemned: *miserorum damnatorumque solatia;* but yet they all remain for him good and beautiful, and in particular, this *natura mentis humanae,* or nature of the human mind, where, even after the fall a living reflection of the creative light still shines.

It is only in the work of the Reformers, and especially of Luther that we see this last reflection obliterated. Still it is proper to observe due prudence even when speaking of a doctrine as intransigent as his. For example, it would be untrue to say that Luther denied purely and simply the persistence of a natural order even after original sin, or that he was completely insensible to what this order has retained of proper value. His opinion on this question is quite apparent in what he has to say of free will, for this characteristic of the will subsists or vanishes with the nature itself, as does knowledge which is the characteristic of the reason. Luther never held that sin had deprived us of the faculty of choosing freely, for, said he, that is only one with the will itself. There is in the will an essential spontaneity that nothing can eliminate. If then by free will is understood the absence of constraint, it is clear that in no case does the will cease to be free, and it is freely, spontaneously, that the just will good under the pressure of grace, as do the wicked will evil under that of concupiscence. Suppose the contrary, submit volition to what the scholastics call *necessitas a coactione,* you make of it a Nolition.[10]

Furthermore, Luther did not contest the evident fact, that man remained free to choose between a multitude of possible acts, as of standing or sitting, of going out wearing a hat or taking a walk bare-headed. We retain our free will with regard to everything below us, that is to say, everything which concerns neither God nor our salvation. In this inferior order, the will is not only free of constraint, as it always is, it is free even of necessity. Let us add, however, that the liberty of man ends there. *"Caeterum erga Deum, vel in rebus quae pertinent ad salutem vel damnationem, non habet liberum arbitrium, sed captivus, subjectus et servus est (homo), vel voluntatis Dei vel voluntatis satanae".*[11]

First of all, therefore, it must be well understood that the Lutheran negation does not deal with nature but with the religious value and efficacy of fallen nature; and secondly that the negation of nature is irrevocable, absolute, and total within these precise limits. That this is so can be

clearly seen from the attitude adopted by Luther in the face
of the classical objection: do not man and God, then, cooperate in the work of salvation? For Catholic theologians,
of whom Erasmus set himself up as spokesman, since man
cooperates, he therefore contributes something to his salvation. For Luther, since God's cooperation is necessary, man
therefore can do nothing to save himself. Nothing, not
even while cooperating.[12] For Luther does not deny that
he does cooperate; quite to the contrary, man can no more
not cooperate with grace if God gives it to him than he can
cooperate with it if God refuses it to him; but that is precisely why his cooperation has absolutely no meritorious
value. Even under the influence of grace which saves it, the
will remains stricken with a total religious sterility, like the
fallen nature of which it is the expression.

What is true of the will is also true of the reason, and
in virtue of the same principle. Luther never committed
the absurdity of denying that there existed in man a natural
light of reason, nor that it remained capable of progressively
constructing a philosophical or scientific interpretation of the
world. He detested Aristotle but admired the philosophy
of Cicero, whose salvation even he hoped for.[13] It is nevertheless still true that anything devoid of religious value
seems to have ceased to interest him. Perhaps there were
still people who were interested in such things; indeed there
were only too many of them; and nothing could convince
them that they were diverted by these things from the one
thing necessary. After all, filth does exist; one can then, if
one loves filth, choose it as a theme for rhetorical exercise.
That is what physics is. As for the true Christian, although
he does not deny that reason, as well as will, has preserved
power over what is below man, yet he remembers that what

it can accomplish is without any true importance, and that it can do nothing whatever about anything really important; anything, that is to say, that concerns God and our salvation. Once again, therefore, it is necessary to maintain that the religious efficacy of nature is nil. Erasmus, who did not understand Luther as well as Luther understood him, thought he had triumphed over his adversary on this point by reminding him of that famous text of the Psalms: *Signatum est super nos lumen vultus tui, Domine.* That was to miss the point as completely as he had done in adducing divine cooperation. For after all, replied Luther to Erasmus, this word which you apply to blind reason refers to the knowledge of the vision itself of God. And what is that knowledge, except faith?[14]

Thus completely disqualified to speak of God in its own right, reason without faith "is of no use, is capable of nothing and might even be harmful". With faith, it is exactly the same reason as before, just as the tongue which praises God is exactly the same as that which blasphemed Him; if then it is able to render any service, it is not that it has become other, but simply that instead of being possessed by the devil it is henceforth enslaved to God.[15] Here then, it is not simply the question, as with Saint Peter Damiani, of knowing whether the natural knowledge of things is dangerous, but indeed whether natural knowledge of God is possible. Luther answers in the negative. Once this irrevocable condemnation was levelled at natural theology, he could fully justify it by the total inaptitude for God with which he had stamped fallen nature. It is impossible, it seems to me, to deny the abstract purity of his position.

To damn philosophy is one way of getting rid of it. It is, however, not the only one, nor the most amiable.

There is notably one other, which was also followed at an early date by Christians, and which consists in transforming it, in sublimating it, so to speak, by incorporating it into the faith, wherein it will of course lose itself just as surely as in the corruption of nature. Reduced to its simplest formula the process usually amounts to this. The world wants a philosophy and a wisdom; it must therefore be given one. Why not offer it the folly of the cross under the name of wisdom? The faith has nothing to lose by it and indeed what it can profit thereby is quite evident. That is why Justin Martyr and Athenagoras, in the 2nd century, and later on, Clement of Alexandria and Augustine, did not scruple to speak of "our" philosophy, or of the "philosophy and wisdom of Christians", to designate what was really supernatural Christian wisdom. The monumental treatise of the Benedictine, Rupert of Deutz, on *Philosophia christiana*, in the 12th century; the *Adhoratio ad studium philosophiae christianae* of Erasmus, in the 16th century, are works of pure theology and, in the latter case, a solemn protest against all Christian philosophy in which reason would pretend to add anything whatever to the Gospel. Here again there was a reformer to appropriate both that Catholic formula and the very attitude which it expressed, but he gave to the formula a new meaning and carried the attitude to its most extreme implications.

In fact it suffices to open the *Institution of the Christian Religion* to find Calvin using this expression on the very first page of his book.[16] What does it signify? The aim which he is pursuing in this work is to teach "the sum total of what God wished to teach us in His word". That is something that can be done only by having recourse to the Scriptures, deposit of the divine word, and "by treating the principal matters of consequence which are contained in Christian philosophy". There then, is philosophy once again reduced to the Word of God, and, that in a manner, as we shall soon see, just as radical as in Luther, though in quite a different spirit. What must be understood above all is that there remains nothing common except the name between the "Christian philosophy" of Calvin and that of Catholic authors, be it that of Erasmus himself, from whom, however, Calvin seems to have borrowed the formula.

For anyone who would study this problem in detail, as indeed it deserves to be studied, I could not insist too much on the use of the same prudence as in analyzing the texts of Luther. The need is even greater here, since the thought of Calvin seems to me more supple than that of the German reformer. Yet, however careful he may have been in expressing his thought, he never was tempted to compromise with what he held to be an absolute theological truth, and these two traits give to his doctrine a complexity that any analysis is bound to respect.

Let us note at the very start, as one of the most striking marks of authentic Calvinism—by which I mean that of Calvin himself—a remarkable insistence on the intrinsic value, the beauty, and in a sense, the excellence of nature even after the fall. This "eulogy of fallen nature" I have already pointed out in Saint Augustine. Now though I would not make bold to assert its complete absence in Luther, I can at least say I have been unable to find it there, and it seems to me to be foreign to his thought. With Calvin, however, its imminent presence is felt from the very beginning of the *Christian institution,* and in each sentence he calls to it with such insistence that indeed it finally appears outright. It is not once, nor twice, but many times and with the most evident sincerity, that the author of the *Institution* "places beyond doubt the fact that there is in the human mind, by a natural inclination, some impression of divinity". All peoples, even the most barbarian, have "this impression in their heart, that there is some God".[17] If you wish, we will call this universal conception,[18] "the seed of religion". At any rate it is sufficient to give us the strict duty of seeking God, and of revering Him in His majesty, and of serving Him. Furthermore, not a single one of the sciences invented by man is incapable on occasion of aiding us in this research; astronomy, medicine, physics, are so many disciplines whose arguments, difficult to understand, are certainly not necessary, but the use of which Calvin nevertheless intimates is lawful.[19] Finally, taken in themselves and apart from their possible usefulness for theology, these works of reason preserve a value of their own, the excellence of which Calvin never allows himself to be swept into misconceiving.

For him, the principle which dominates the whole problem is a distinction: that, namely, which must be introduced between "the understanding of terrestrial things" and the understanding of "things celestial".[20] He seems, therefore, to have extended to the problem of knowledge what Luther had already said with regard to free will, and not without reason, since science and liberty are two different manifestations of one and the same nature, two evidences of the status wherein they are found. What are the "things terrestrial"? Those which "do not concern God and His kingdom, nor true justice and the immortality of the future life, but are wedded to the present life, and, so to speak, enclosed within its limits." Thus man is and remains qualified to exercise the so called liberal disciplines; literature, the diverse arts, medicine, law, philosophy, as so many evidences of the divine light which shines in man and will never cease to shine in him. It is by this distinction that Calvin logically justifies the sympathy for profane culture which he discloses, in contrast with the active enmity against it so frequently expressed in the writings of Luther. For indeed, he asks us, "when we see in pagan writers the admirable light of truth, that appeared in their works", does it not proclaim to us, "that the nature of man, however much it has fallen from its integrity, and been corrupted, is nevertheless still embellished by many gifts of God"? "If we recognize the Spirit of God as the one unique fountain of truth, we will not despise truth wherever it appears, unless we would want to wrong the Spirit of God. For the gifts of the Spirit cannot be defamed without scorning and reproaching the Spirit Himself". In short, "we must esteem nothing excellent or laudable, which we do not recognize as coming from God".[21]

Is this not a return to Augustine with his untiring avowal of admiration for the ancients? Are we not listening to Justin Martyr: all that is true and beautiful is ours? Or, what is still more strange, has not Calvin rejoined Berengarius of Tours, when he goes so far as to write: "If the Lord wished that the iniquitous and the infidels should help us to understand physics, dialectics and the other disciplines, we must use them in those things, lest our negligence be punished, should we despise the gifts of God wherever they are presented to us".[22] Although Luther never condemned the moderate use of at least an extremely simplified dialectics, he would certainly not make of it a grace of the Holy Ghost, or a divine gift. But let us not forget what rigorous limits Calvin himself wishes to impose on the natural powers

of fallen reason: never can it flatter itself with even the least
competence, when it is a question of God or of the future
life. Much more supple than Luther, he is no less firm than
him in this conclusion; yet he cannot maintain it without
overcoming many difficulties.

Like all theologians of the Middle Ages, Calvin had to
take a stand on the formula of Saint Paul, so often quoted
by Saint Bonaventure, Saint Thomas and many others:
"What it is necessary to know of God hath been manifested,
for the invisible things of Him, even His eternal power
and divinity, are evident when considered from the creation
of the world".[23] But to what knowledge does this refer?
Not, evidently, knowledge of the divine essence, which remains for us "hidden"; it refers only to that knowledge of
the "powers" of God, which the world reveals to us to the
extent that is necessary for our salvation; His glory first,
then His wisdom, power, goodness, providence and mercy.
Knowledge less speculative than experimental and sensible.
Besides, adds Calvin, Saint Paul "teaching that what must
be known of God is manifested by the creation of the world,
does not mean a manifestation of a sort that may be compre-
hended by the human understanding, but rather suggests
that it does not go beyond making men inexcusable".[24] If,
therefore, this natural blindness is dissipated, whence comes
the light to us? From reason? By no means. The little
natural light that remains in us now throws out but feeble
sparks, which are extinguished as soon as they spurt forth.
Just as we must recognize ourselves bare of all virtue in
order to be clothed by God, enslaved by sin in order to be
delivered by God, so also must we confess ourselves "blind,
in order to be enlightened". And let not our adversaries,
adds Calvin, start to object, saying that, by this means,

"would be subverted even the blind light of nature",[25] for man is truly blind in regard to everything which is of God and the future life. In the face of such problems, he is really but "half-alive"; and let us be sure that the half of man which is dead, that which ought to be turned towards God to confess His existence and revere His majesty, is completely dead: "Let this sentence which is absolutely unshakable, remain firm and certain for us, namely, that the understanding of man is so far alienated from the justice of God, that it cannot imagine, conceive, nor understand anything save perverseness, iniquity and corruption". The only light which can enlighten us in these matters, is, therefore, faith in the divine word. This faith, which will be *in* the understanding without its light ever being *of* the understanding, does not leave it less blind in itself than grace leaves our free will helpless. If perchance there comes from man "something which would appear good", his reason for all that remains "always enveloped in hypocrisy and vanity" as his heart remains "addicted to every malice".[26] Thus, founded on the word of God, worked out quite entirely within by the light of faith, and by it alone, the "Christian philosophy" of Calvin is a purely supernatural knowledge; in a word it is a theology.

Nothing better than such a fact discloses what radical diversity of thought can be hidden under the identity of the formulae which express them. On one side, the reformer Calvin makes use of the name "Christian philosophy", which the Catholic Erasmus had just brought into or restored to fashion. In fact, both agree to make it a theology, and even a theology in which the Reformer would welcome dialectics more generously perhaps than would the Catholic. The position of Calvin, however, differs profoundly from that of

Erasmus, inasmuch as it is pure and coherent, whereas that of Erasmus is not. For the fundamental question is to know what remains of nature. Is our natural light irremediably blind to God and to everything which is of God or not? Calvin answers affirmatively; he has, therefore, the right to conclude that all natural theology as such is impossible. Erasmus, the Catholic, has to answer in the negative; but then by what right does he pretend to condemn as sterile or harmful all effort of natural reason to investigate things divine?

This inconsistency, which Luther took for treason, is precisely what the Reformers never excused in him. The reduction of Christian philosophy to a pure theology can be only a simple attitude in which is expressed, with a profound recognition of the gift of Revelation and an exalted respect for the light of faith, a certain mistrust in regard to reason as soon as it takes God for its object. Many famous Catholic doctors have lived in such an opinion, and doubtless still many more unknown ones, who remained silent on this matter. As a practical attitude, this reduction of philosophy to theology is no more difficult to understand than the condemnation of all philosophy by the "spirituals" of the Middle Ages. Fundamentally, it is the same preoccupation which is expressed thus by two different temperaments. It is quite otherwise with the Reformers. With them, the conditions required for these simple attitudes to be doctrinally founded immediately come to the fore. If you sincerely condemn philosophy as harmful, says Luther to Erasmus, then admit first that the nature which it interprets is irremediably corrupted. If you sincerely recommend a "Christian philosophy", says Calvin to Erasmus, then admit that reason contributes nothing to it, and that it is exclusively the work of faith. But the Catholic humanist could deny neither the nature which grace healed, nor the natural light to which faith restored sight. And for me to add that I side with him on that point will be no news to you. But then what business had he to attack philosophy? Since he was anxious to maintain an order of nature endowed with some religious efficacy, Erasmus had no right to reduce natural theology to faith. Evidently of the two Calvin alone had a right to do so.

To discover an attitude other than that of the Reformers, and at the same time coherent, we cannot then look to the Catholic "spirituals" nor to the Catholic "humanists". The true masters in this matter can only be those great Catholic theologians, who were at the same time profound philosophers, and who fully recognized that, as Catholics, they had to be both the one and the other. Though differing in temperament, they all pursued the study of the problem up to the point of attaining its ultimate foundation. Here again the formulae signify nothing apart from the sense that was given them. Compare, for example, the beginning of two celebrated treatises. "The whole sum of our wisdom, which deserves to be called true and certain wisdom, is as it were composed of two parts, in having a knowledge of God, and of ourselves". This is the first sentence of the *Institution* of J. Calvin. "Wisdom consists in knowing God and in knowing oneself"; that is the first sentence of the treatise, *Of the knowledge of God and of self,* of Jacques-Bénigne Bossuet. Does anyone imagine that these two men wished to do and say the same thing? In reality, the whole *Institution* is a work of theology, the whole treatise of Bossuet is a work of philosophy: Calvin referred entirely to faith, Bossuet solely to reason, and while the first work has no other purpose than to reveal the divine majesty by the word of God, the second quietly attains "to the conclusion of this treatise in which the excellence of human nature is again demonstrated". Yet, Calvin cannot be accused of ignoring philosophy nor Bossuet theology. The radical difference which separates these two works, identical in their programs, is the very difference which separates the Protestant from the Catholic.

For there is also an essential purity in the Catholic position, which, however, is not more easily attained than that of the Protestant position, and perhaps even less, since it consists in the respect of an order, instead of resulting from a simplification. That it is difficult to grasp and still more to retain, is evident from the controversies which have recently risen among Catholic historians, philosophers and theologians on the very possibility of a Christian philosophy. Were it not for the habitual instability of man and his tendency to live in compromise, this might be surprising. For, in the last analysis, taken in itself, the Catholic position ought to be clear at least for Catholics, since on this point, it reduces itself to what is so well expressed by the concise formula of Erasmus: *instauratio bene conditae naturae.* That nature was created good, Catholics and Protestants alike agree. The danger which besets the Protestant is either straight Manicheanism, which is a corruption of the very principle of the Reform, or a certain liberalism, which is its abandonment. The danger which besets the Catholic is a semi-calvinism, which leads him to despair of nature, or a semi-pelagianism, which invites him to do without grace. The true Catholic position consists in maintaining that nature was created good, that it has been wounded, but that it can be at least partially healed by grace if God so wishes. This *instauratio,* that is to say, this renewal, this re-establishment, this restoration of nature to its primitive goodness by grace, is on this point the program of authentic Catholicism.

If such is the case, who does not see that a "Christian philosophy" is possible in Catholicism, that it is even necessary there, and that only there is it possible and necessary? It is first of all possible there, if we understand by this formula a true philosophy which is the work of natural reason as such, and not some theological substitute for a natural knowledge of God and of the soul, which should henceforth be considered impossible. For St. Thomas Aquinas makes of philosophy a work of natural reason, the *perfectum opus rationis*, which is constructed in the light of the intellect and its principles, not in that of faith. Furthermore, it must be conceded that, in the doctrine of St. Thomas Aquinas, the acumen of human reason has much less suffered from original sin than the rectitude of the will. Yet it did suffer, and since it is a work of fallen nature, natural theology bears inevitably the marks of this decadence. Already prevented from yielding its full fruit even when it stoops to things below it, our wounded reason is indeed still more so, when it attempts to raise itself to God. In order that it may succeed in this, in the measure permitted by its natural perfection, grace must first purify it, dress its wounds and guide it towards an object of which it is no longer worthy; but as soon as grace does this, it is indeed the withered reason itself, which revives under grace, the same reason, but healed, saved, therefore in another state, which sees and proves. Its knowledge is therefore truly natural, its philosophy even though christianized is a true philosophy.

Against this manner of conceiving and designating the speculative activity of reason, objections are not lacking, even among Catholics. Just, however, as I understand that it ought to be completely rejected by a Protestant, so it is difficult for me to see what a Catholic can take exception to in it. We are told that since there is no "Christian science" it is hard to see why or how there should be a "Christian philosophy." That there may not be any "Christian science" is possible, but perhaps it is regrettable, for there ought to be one, were it only to maintain science in its proper order, which is that of contemplation, and prevent it from sinking into that of practical application, where it loses its proper essence without benefit to religion or to reason. But above all, since it is impossible to treat this problem fully here, let us say that the case of philosophy is not that of any other science, because it cannot be completed without a metaphysic, nor can a metaphysic be completed without a natural theology. If natural reason, the image of God in man, is still and cannot but remain *capax Dei* in the order of knowledge, it is certainly no longer *capax* in the same way as before the fall, and its light can only with difficulty rediscover God without error unless that of faith is added to it. Indeed even if one persists in maintaining that revelation of God, the Lord of all knowledge (*Deus scientiarum Dominus*)[27] is of no use in the natural sciences, there will still remain the problem of knowing whether the reason of a human nature weakened by the fall, cannot be helped by grace in its effort to know God.

The second most frequent objection is that if faith is required to enlighten reason, then we leave philosophy to take up theology. In short, though wishing to avoid it, we return in spite of ourselves to that type of "Christian philosophy" which consists in suppressing philosophy under the pretext of better saving it. I do not think that is true. The truth of the matter is that the expression and the very notion of "Christian philosophy" denotes a theological view of philosophy, but it does not follow from that, that the philosophy thus conceived be itself a theology.   To say that grace is necessary to restore nature is quite other than to suppress that nature to the profit of grace: it is to confirm it by grace. Grace presupposes nature, whether to restore or to enrich it. When grace restores nature, it does not substitute itself for it, but re-establishes it; when nature, thus re-established by grace, accomplishes its proper operations, they are indeed natural operations which it performs.   Could a Catholic maintain that what nature cannot do without grace is no longer done by nature at all?   Far from it, no one could maintain such a thesis without endangering the very foundations of the Catholic order and of becoming involved in serious difficulties.   What would be done with natural morals?   Would one say that the effect of grace is to suppress natural morals rather than re-establish them?   Or, to avoid this consequence, would one go so far as to hold that the natural moral order does not come under the influence of grace?   And then what should we do in theology itself when we have to come to the thorny problem of merit? For if nature owes all its merit to grace, it is nevertheless that nature which merits—by grace: "Man", says St. Thomas emphatically, "merits in so far as it is by his own will that he does what he ought".[28]   What is true of the order of the will is also true, and in virtue of the same principle, of the order of knowledge.   Just as, therefore, there is a natural morality re-established by grace, there can and ought to be a natural theology restored by faith.   In this sense, since Catholicism holds for a nature which can be healed, it maintains the possibility of a philosophy; but since in fact this natural theology can hardly be established validly without the aid of faith, it

will be Christian or will run the great risk of being only a
false philosophy. That is why I said that "Christian philosophy" is not only possible in Catholicism, but that it is
indispensable to it. And I admit that such a view of the
question is theological. I even consent to being excluded
from philosophy for taking this theological view; to be quite
precise, I consent to it in two cases: if my judge is a Protestant who, because he keeps faith with his own principles, denies the validity of all natural theology; or if he is a pagan
who denies the possibility of all supernatural revelation.
But if my critic is a Catholic, I am reduced to supposing that
one of us is mistaken as to the essence of Catholicism, the sort
of question that is seldom profitable to settle single handed.

The conclusion to be derived from this analysis is that
if faith is essentially a gift of God, the man who thinks so
has at least the duty of accepting frankly, completely and
without restrictions the consequences of the new situation in
which this gift places him. The greatest of all blessings
would be for all of us to live in the unity of the same faith.
Since we have lost that great good, we must content ourselves
provisionally with the lesser evil, which is for Protestants,
to think as Protestants, Catholics, to think truly as Catholics. Such is at least the fundamental condition in order
that we may understand each other and listen to each other,
for want of being united. For union can in no case be effected
in confusion, and, while waiting for the accomplishment of
this union, nothing can hasten its coming more than clarity
and straightforwardness. It is certainly fitting that each of
us seize on everything which, in the other, is really an infi-
delity to the truth which he claims; it is, however, with this
truth alone that we are concerned, not with what he says
about it or does with it. When we judge it, it is for fear

that it will judge us. To avoid such weaknesses, let us, therefore, help one another to know what this truth is, rather than criticize what we do with it. It is perhaps not an enviable privilege for us to have to posit these problems for ourselves, but how can we get around the fact that they are there, once they have put in an appearance? There is no middle course between not thinking of these things at all and thinking them out to the very end. There is no middle course, once one thinks of them, between knowing what Catholicism and Protestantism are and not knowing why one is himself Protestant or Catholic. I do not pretend to have succeeded in this matter but it is in this spirit at least that I wished to reply to your appeal. Instead of choosing for you, and that I am not free to do; or of choosing for myself, and that, I hope, I am no longer free to do, I have only wished to consider before you the inevitable consequences of our choice and the attitude it imposes on us, if, at least, we mean to remain faithful to our truth.

II

CALVINISM AND PHILOSOPHY

THE mere profession of a doctrine is much easier than the actual compliance of one's thought to it. Nor do the Calvinists escape from this law, especially when their effort to be reunited to the true thought of Calvin becomes more intense. Some of them seem to experience a repugnance in sacrificing natural theology, not however, without perceiving how difficult it is for an authentic Calvinist to maintain a reality corresponding to that term. In this sense the attempt of A. Lecerf seems to me to be one of the most instructive that has been made. Because of the sincerity, the integrity of thought, as well as the painstaking distinctions revealed in it, it assuredly merits attention.

The first thing to notice is that for a Calvinistic theologian the problem of philosophy can be stated only as a consequence of faith; but this principle itself gives rise to consequences which vary according to its different applications. What place ought philosophy to hold in relation to faith? The first answer would consist in making it a sort of propaedeutic or an "introduction to the study of dogmas", which would itself be a "philosophy of faith by faith".[1] Clearly, however, this answer raises another question, namely, what is a philosophy of faith? Taken in its literal sense, this expression can only signify a reduction of faith to the rules of natural reason, in which case we certainly have a philos-

27

ophy but no longer a faith; or, on the contrary, it can signify an invitation to reason to enter into the realm of faith
with a view to investigating its mystery, in which case we
can indeed maintain faith, but we are certain to lose philosophy understood as the natural exercise of pure reason. In
short it becomes a question of knowing whether we want
to confine religion within the limits of reason, or reason
within the limits of revelation?

To this second question, there can be no doubt as to the
Calvinistic answer: clearly it is a question of subjecting reason to faith, or to be more precise, of forbidding reason to
speak in terms other than those of faith. Doubtless, we
still have a knowledge, and a true thought but it is a "religious knowledge", and a "religious thought", which plainly
presuppose faith as their basis and starting-point. Both in
the case of dogmatic theology properly so called, and of
that introduction to dogmatic theology, which would be
philosophy, the *Credo ut intelligam* of Saint Anselm is
equally incumbent, since "in both it is a question of understanding what is already known by faith".[2] A classical
position, indeed, inasmuch as it refers to one of the undis-
puted masters of Christian thought in the Middle Ages, but
one of which the philosophical value may be questioned.
We might even legitimately ask, moreover, what meaning
the formula will have as the accurate definition of a theological position. For after all, to say that "the rôle of the
speculative reason in theology is limited to the understanding
of revelation",[3] is to leave in doubt the exact connotation
given to the word "understand", and it is by no means certain that a Calvinistic theologian can give it the same meaning
that Saint Anselm did. That is the first point on which

we can usefully pause before proceeding further, since it touches the very heart of the question.

We know indeed that it is an effort to introduce *necessary* reasons into faith which characterizes Saint Anselm's position; necessary in the sense that they are logically compulsory and make the contrary appear intellectually *impossible*. There is no rationalism in the position, since in it faith precedes the activity of reason whose object it becomes, accompanies the effort of reason, but remains completely independent of it, not having to wait for the rational proof, which is neither its foundation nor even its confirmation in any sense whatever. But we must still ask whether a Calvinistic dogmatic theology which appeals to the formula of Saint Anselm is authorized in understanding the *intellectus* of faith in this sense, without betraying its own principles?

We are not told that it is so and there are reasons for doubting it. St. Thomas himself did not dare go that far. Rather, let us say that he formally denied, against Anselm and Richard of Saint Victor, the possibility of introducing into theology necessary demonstrations of such mysteries as the Trinity or the Incarnation. Indeed, the most common reproach respectfully addressed to Saint Anselm by Catholic historians or theologians is that of having "skirted rationalism" or of having fallen, though involuntarily, into a sort of "Christian rationalism". Although this accusation seems to me to be unfounded, it nevertheless gives cause for reflection. Be that as it may, if we stick to the purely dogmatic reserve formulated by Saint Thomas, it seems clear that whatever Thomism condemns as an excessive pretension of reason in matters of faith, ought to appear still more unacceptable from the point of view of authentic Calvinism. Difficult though it be for an outsider to say just how reformed dogmatic theology would criticize the real doctrine of Saint Anselm, yet it seems probable that it would reproach it for having substituted, were it only provisionally, a purely intellectual contemplation of the rational necessity of faith, for the pure acceptation of faith itself. Saint Anselm, we know, placed his *intellectus* of faith between blind faith and the beatific vision; but not only is the divine word and the adherence of the soul to this word by faith the proper object of Calvinistic dogmatic theology, it is its very substance. Saint Thomas regards any attempt to prove or rationally to demonstrate a mystery as a blow aimed at the transcendence of faith; authentic Calvinism would doubtless see in it, above all, the introduction of a rational substitute between the word of God and faith; a substitute, which, if it does not pretend to establish faith in right, at least dispenses us from it in fact. The majesty of God requires our attention, not our understanding; that man bow down before its necessity, not seize hold of it and place himself on a level with it by proving it. The *intellectus* of Saint Anselm which flatters itself with demonstrating *the same thing* that Scripture teaches without quoting Scripture, is an eminently Catholic phenomenon on account of the confidence it expresses in the resources of natural reason. For a Calvinist it is to be feared that it would be an offense against the divine dignity; the gravest, as well as the most common of crimes. In no case could it be the definition of theology for him.

Nor can it be the definition of philosophy for anyone at all. If by this term is to be understood a speculation of the natural reason on objects which are accessible to it in the state of fact natural to it, the decision, taken once for all to concentrate its efforts on the contents of the Christian faith, suffices to place outside the philosophical field anything the reason, so engaged, has to say. In fact when we are told that "the rôle of the speculative reason in theology is limited to understanding revelation, drawing inferences from principles, organizing, and finally criticizing contradictory formulae",[4] it is apparent that the "philosophy *of* faith *by* faith" in question, moves entirely on a plane transcendent to that of pure reason. It is not a philosophy, but a theology.

A mere question of words, you may say. Perhaps! But that is not so sure. When a theologian, condemned by his very principles to have only a theology, still speaks of philosophy, the mere survival of the word in his vocabulary is an indication, if not of a defection, at least of a temptation. Even if it were only a question of a mere tendency, still it would be worth the trouble of explaining it, nor is it difficult to discover what renders its presence comprehensible in a truly Calvinistic thought.

The theological error hated above all others by reformed dogmatic theology is the pretension, which it generally ascribes to Scholasticism, of giving a "rational foundation to revealed theology".[5] That, we might note in passing, is an excellent example of those reproaches flung at each other by both sides, which have no other effect than to perpetuate the schism from which the Church suffers, by substituting pseudo-oppositions for real oppositions. It is easy to write that Scholasticism "wishes to have us find God *at the end* of its syllogisms and to constitute a speculative science of the divine essence", but how would it be proven? Neither for Saint Anselm, nor for Saint Bonaventure, Saint Thomas Aquinas, Saint Albert the Great, Duns Scotus, Occam, nor, in a word, for any of the great masters of scholastic theology, would the pretension of finding God by this means have any sense. Their critic is mistaken here about the *end* and in his desire that theirs be not the same as his, he forgets that all scholastic theology claims to be theology, precisely because it is founded on the word of God, and on nothing else. A *scientia?* Certainly, but, as Saint Thomas says in the very first article of the *Summa Theologica*, a science inspired of God (*scientia divinitus inspirata*), about which he adds that, for this very reason, it does not belong to the philosophical disciplines which have been constructed by human reason (*non pertinet ad philosophicas disciplinas, quae sunt secundum rationem humanam inventae*). The end from which scholastic theology takes its start is not natural reason armed with its principles, but indeed the *articuli fidei,* and that towards which it tends is not an evacuation of the mystery, but the submission of the intellect to the mystery of Christ: "bringing into captivity every understanding unto the obedience of Christ".[6] For Saint Thomas can also cite Saint Paul [7] and it is on this very point that he quotes this text. What so profound a Catholic theologian affirms so vigorously cannot but express a common Catholic position; and if proving it is a waste of time, what then would denying it be?

That, therefore, is not and cannot be the essential difference between Calvinism and Catholicism on this point. To say that "a faith created by scientific demonstration would not be faith, but a science, probably a pseudo-science", is not raising an objection against the scholastic theologians, but is only echoing them. The real difficulty begins when one adds: "On the other hand, a faith that reasoning has dissolved, was not faith, it was a rational counterfeit of it; faith is stable".[8] For it is clear that here the objection seems partly to apply, if not to all the scholastics (for Saint Bonaventure, Duns Scotus, and Occam go rather far in this direction), at least to Saint Thomas Aquinas, whose doctrine is the norm of Catholic theology. It is quite true that, for a Thomist theologian, there are some revealed truths which are and will always remain impenetrable to the reason, others which on the contrary are intelligible to it. The dogma of the Trinity is the classic example of the first category, the existence of God is the typical instance of the second. But Saint Thomas teaches that one cannot, at the same time and under the same aspect, believe and know the same thing. If anyone, who once believed in the existence of God on the testimony of God Himself, succeeds in proving it for himself, he will then know that God exists and inasmuch as he knows it, he will no longer believe it. His faith, at least on this point, would not therefore be "stable". It remains to be seen whether it was only a rational counterfeit; but if such a judgment is pressed ever so little the disproportion between the sentence of the convicting judge and the validity of the grounds soon appears.

To tell the truth, such grounds do not exist. In order to criticize them we must first imagine them, for we are told absolutely nothing of the facts alleged by Thomist theologians for establishing the position for which they are reproached. But the strangest thing about it is that these facts are so evident that reformed dogmatic theology finds itself at grips with them, not without wondering where and how it will be able to make room for them.

It would make the matter simple if we were to consider the doctrine of Saint Thomas as a rational crisis which arose more or less suddenly about the middle of the 13th century. Before judging the ideas it contains, it is always useful to take into consideration the realities it proposes to interpret. In the present instance, the reality about which both Saint Thomas and Calvin can do nothing, is that the notion of God and that of a religious cult are both anterior to Christianity, that they are found even among all the so-called pagan peoples, and that consequently a problem arises as to their origin. The first treatment of this important fact appears in the doctrine of Saint Paul. We have already seen how Calvin interprets his texts on this point, and this is not the place to discuss his exegesis, but it may at least be remarked that these texts do exist and that Calvinism has therefore the duty of interpreting them. What is this knowledge of the *invisibilia Dei* that man can obtain from a consideration of creation? What does the Apostle mean, when he speaks of those pagans who, not having the Law, "accomplish naturally what the Law commands" because "what the Law commands is written in their hearts"? In whatever way these texts of the *Epistle to the Romans* may be understood, they suffice to show that Saint Paul is think-ing of those who *"having known God,* do not glorify Him as God",[9] a fact of such importance that it cannot be sup-pressed without ruining his whole doctrine. It is because, having known God, they did not glorify Him as God, that the pagans are inexcusable. To forget that men "read in themselves what can be known of God", since His eternal power and His divinity "are rendered visible to the intelli-gence by means of His works", is to nullify the chief accu-sation against the pagans, which justifies the divine anger, and to render useless the redemption of the gentiles. There were then a Greek religion, a Roman religion, a Greek philos-ophy and a Roman philosophy; Saint Paul knew it, for he was a contemporary. Saint Thomas and Calvin knew it, just as we do, from history, and there is no Christian theology but what owes it to itself to offer some explanation of the fact.

Saint Thomas' explanation is simple. For him there can be no doubt as to the reality itself of the fact to be explained. Saint Paul had expressly attributed to the pagans a natural knowledge of God; he himself, in the course of his patient and careful study of Aristotle, had been convinced that the Apostle told the truth. It is easy for us today to perceive how imperfect was the natural theology of the greatest Greek philosophers when compared to the revealed theology of Christianity. Catholic doctors have not been lacking who emphasized its insufficiencies and even despised it. But Saint Thomas never thought that to despise creation, even for the purpose of exalting revelation, was an homage pleasing to God. What the Creator adds does not detract from what He gives, and what He gave to the profound intellect of Plato and Aristotle was already sufficient to merit the most fervent thanksgiving.

The heritage of Greek thought, even when cut to the minimum and judged most critically, is still worthy of admiration. So true is this that a number of the Fathers were convinced that the pagan thinkers had access to the Bible without admitting it. One first being, the supreme principle and cause of nature, source of all intelligibility, of all order, and of all beauty, who eternally leads a life of happiness, because, being thought itself, it is an eternal contemplation of its own thought, all that was taught by Aristotle; and if we compare his theology to the ancient mythologies we will see at a glance what immense progress human reason had made since the era of Chronos and Jupiter without the aid of Christian Revelation. Doubtless there were many lacunae, and numberless errors mingled with these truths. But they were still truths. Discovered by the natural reason of the Greeks, they owed nothing to faith; still discoverable today, with even greater ease, by the same natural reason, why should they owe more to faith in our own reason than in Aristotle's? Furthermore, if like him we know what Aristotle knew about God without faith, and for the same reasons or for other reasons as cogent as his, how would we accept Him, at one time and under the same aspect, both because of the rational evidence which enlightens us and the divine word which teaches it? Reason cannot have been blinded nor weakened by the light of Revelation; the teaching of Scripture could not render us less capable of finding God than were the pagans. That is all that Saint Thomas said, and that is what anyone, wishing to censure him, would have to criticize; but above all it is that to which anyone must first be able to become adjusted, before attempting to criticize him.

The thesis under discussion is in reality reduced to the analysis of a few definite facts. Reason, having formerly been capable of finding out certain truths about God, ought to be still able to do so today, at least among those who have the leisure, the desire and the ability to carry such researches to a successful conclusion. Nowadays, just as in Aristotle's time, those fulfilling these several conditions are relatively few; God, desiring the salvation of all, has therefore revealed to all even those salutary truths which some men formerly discovered by reason alone. Those who rediscover them on their own account know them, from the moment they so discover them. The rest believe them, as every Christian does in the beginning, whether or not he be destined to become one day a philosopher. Before condemning as a "rational counterfeit" of faith that which the Catholic Church commends, we will have to know what is to be substituted for it. Before dogmatically laying down as an evident principle that "faith is stable", we will have to know if whatever remains of reason in man after the fall is unstable. In other words we must determine whether the first effect of Christian Revelation has been to strip us of whatever remained of natural reason in Plato and Aristotle. Only when this question has been asked and a suitable answer given, can any opposition be set up against Saint Thomas Aquinas.

The simplest answer would be to say that faith could not blind natural reason, since this reason was already totally blind. That was, as we have already seen, Calvin's reply, and we must reconsider it. But it is not easy, it admits of difficulties and it is natural that its interpreters should colour it according to their personal preferences. To maintain that natural theology is "incapable of establishing religious knowledge" [10] is still to miss the heart of the question, for understanding religious knowledge to be a theology, no Catholic would contest that proposition. The position which it states is, in truth, a Catholic position. The real problem is to determine whether reason alone cannot proceed at least a part, however small, of the way, over which faith takes it the entire distance. Here again equivocation must be carefully avoided. It does not suffice to say that reason alone can attain "a God, but not God", in order to oppose Thomistic doctrine,[11] for Saint Thomas would also find no difficulty in admitting that. Once we understand by "God", the one and only true God, such as is known and adored by the Christian, it follows without saying that no one can know Him without adhering to and complying with the divine word. Never has a Thomist, and still less a Bonaventurian or a Scotist, admitted that the God accessible to reason was God—one in three Persons, and Jesus Christ, Who became

Man, suffered under Pontius Pilate and died on the cross to save us. What Catholic theology does maintain is that reason by itself can discover *a* God, and that this God which it discovers is already the true God, precisely because there is no other, and that whatever truth we know about God can consequently apply to Him alone.

This may not be very much, but it is something and is not negligible. No one could treat it as such without admitting that anything at all which the natural reason can say about God is of equal value, whether it is a question of the grossest fetishism, of the materialism of the stoics, of the demiurge of Plato, of the pure thought of Aristotle, or of the One of Plotinus. Besides, to address such a criticism to natural theology is to forget that every Catholic philosopher is, in this regard, in the same boat as the pagan philosopher. Beyond the little that he knows about God there is all that he believes about Him without rational demonstration of it. Faith is for him not only the guide whose hand he holds tightly whenever he is not certain of being in the light; he clutches it even more tightly, so as never to lose his grip, whenever he has to leave the narrow glade of natural theology to enter the dark recesses of mystery. For he knows by his reason that God exists, and that His works resemble Him, but by faith he believes that God is unlike His works and how little indeed His works resemble Him. The more he buries himself in faith, the more God reveals Himself to him according to the words of Saint Thomas, as *magis ac magis elongatus ab his omnibus quae in effectibus apparent.* Nevertheless the God discovered by reason is indeed that very One: the same God seen in the measure in which He permits Himself to be seen. What man is naturally capable of knowing about God, but in fact does not

know and perhaps will never know in this life, he therefore believes just as firmly and as truly as that which he is
naturally incapable of knowing about Him. The beatific
vision will not prevent our faith from having been a true
faith; still less could the light of reason retroactively dis-
qualify the act of faith by which so many men affirm God,
and His Unity, solely on the testimony of His own word.
And finally the light of faith never disqualifies that of reason, but on the contrary guides it until, once having found
faith, it even dares to try to surpass it.

Passing the problem off on Catholics alone is, moreover, simplifying it altogether too much, for it obligates
Calvinists as well, and especially with regard to the existence
of God. Calvin openly made of it a natural knowledge;
would then the Calvinist not believe in God? For after all
there is quite a distance, philosophically speaking, between
positing a God, the Creator of nature, and denying the existence of God in the name of an empiricism clinging to its
negation of everything which is beyond experience. In other
words, the affirmation of the existence of *a* God is a proposition much nearer the truth with respect to the true God
than the pure and simple denial of God's existence. More
than that, how could this knowledge of God be a sufficient
motive for the divine anger, if, by it, man in no wise attained
the true God? Perhaps it is the vague feeling of the im-
possibility of avoiding this problem, which induces certain
Calvinistic theologians to concede that "strictly speaking, it
would not be contrary to dogma to admit the possibility of
demonstrating a god, but not God"; or, at least to admit "as
possible, as far as rational demonstration is concerned, only
the demonstration of the existence of a god, more or less
indetermined, and not that of God".[12] A real concession,

for even if it be granted to Calvin that pagan monotheism has no more religious value than polytheism, nevertheless the same is not true of its philosophical value, even in the eyes of a theologian.[13]   It is necessary, then, that a certain natural theology remain possible, that is to say, a knowledge of God which is not merely an intellection of faith, nor a philosophy of faith by faith, nor, in a word, a supernatural knowledge.   It is hardly necessary to point out that this is simply a return to the scholastic position.   And by the way note also it is not so much a return to Saint Thomas, to whom they are partial, as to Duns Scotus, whom the Calvinists detest,[14] and whom this "strictly speaking" would nevertheless delight.   Duns Scotus would be quite satisfied to hear faith qualified as "stable", and would readily agree that, though reason does attain God, still by itself it cannot know very much about Him.   Catholic theologians could easily be found, who would be content with even less, but having once granted it they would not feel justified in paying no further attention to the little with which they were satisfied. It is just that which separates them radically from Calvinism, and the point is quite important enough to warrant the endeavour to state it precisely.

Once a Calvinistic theologian remembers to uphold a natural knowledge of God, he is quite capable of going rather far along that path, and even of being satisfied with much less effort than a Catholic would be.   For him indeed it is a question of maintaining a natural knowledge of God, only by reducing it to its strict minimum, and eliminating from it as much as possible whatever might make of this natural knowledge of God in man a knowledge of God by man. The simplest way of accomplishing that is to free it from all proof.   That is why Calvin made an innate knowledge of

it, not in order to confer on it an evidence not its own, but
to deprive reason of any pretext for claiming the merit of
it for itself.   In this sense must be understood that stoical
expression of "common notion",[15] found in the writings of
Calvin and those of his disciples, and which he himself borrowed from Seneca, on whom we know he commented.   At
first sight, it would seem that there could not be a better
solution.   But it is still true that this knowledge is confronted by the problem just as certainly as is the rational
certitude which the Thomistic proofs of the existence of God
claim to attain.   Either it is a natural certitude, in which
case the right to criticize the Catholic position and to suppress pure philosophy is lost; or it is a supernatural certitude,
in which case it would become impossible to find a place for
that natural knowledge of God, which is exactly what one
was pretending to conserve.

The attenuations of language will in no way change the
postulates of this problem.   Let us admit, if you will, that
there is only a question here of an "impression of divinity"
as Calvin puts it, and that it may rightly be considered as a
"natural grace", or even as "faith . . . which the human mind,
on contact with experimental reality, forms by a natural
inclination".   Even disregarding the philosophical problems
which underlie such expressions, the theological problem remains.   Since it is natural, this "faith" or "common notion",
or "innate idea", or "religious aptitude, innate in the same
sense as the aptitude for language",[16] in short, this rudiment
of virtual knowledge, whatever be its nature, remains a gift
which man does not owe to Revelation.   If, according to
the formula of Calvin himself, "experience attests that God
has placed in all men an innate seed of religion",[17] we must
necessarily admit that natural reason has some grounds for

speaking about religion and some justification for its efforts to attain God. Is it not precisely on this fundamental notion that philosophers such as Plato and Aristotle have relied, in order to construct their natural theologies and to carry Greek religion far beyond the gross anthropomorphism in which Homer and Hesiod had left it? Can we not in a similar way still acquire whatever knowledge of God, and especially of His existence, that they were able to attain, beginning with the spectacle of creation? If we can still know what Plato and Aristotle knew, then we have no more need of believing it than they did. Neither more, nor less for that matter, and so we are back again where we started.

There is, then, as it were, a Calvinistic antinomy, the solution of which must doubtless be sought on a plane other than that of reason and philosophy, for it is insoluble as long as any shadow of credit is given to nature, and therefore to reason. To tell the truth, even though reformed dogmatic theology continues to speak of philosophy and still manages to have one, nevertheless it really doesn't want one. As far as it is concerned, it is first of all useless to seek God by reason, since we have a spontaneous natural knowledge of Him, which suffices to assure us of His existence; but besides, and this is more important, it is "illegitimate" to seek God by reason, since by nature He has "the right of being believed".[18] This is the exception before which the reason has but to bow, as before an irrevocable religious decree which depends purely on faith. We shall not therefore discuss it; but even while accepting it as it is, we still have a rational request to make of it.

Enclosed as it is within barriers that are rationally impregnable, and willing to remain there, the prohibition which it imposes on itself of philosophizing does not authorize it to condemn the use of philosophy as impossible for all Christian faith. That is a discretion of which reformed dogmatic theology sometimes needs to be reminded. "To establish faith in His existence", M. A. Lecerf concludes, "it ought to be enough for God to disclose Himself; we do not ask anything more for believing in the existence of finite things. *God, therefore, is knowable, in the last analysis, only by the intuition of faith.*" No, this conclusion does not follow from the premises. True, it can be sufficient for God to show Himself to us by faith in order that we may know Him, nevertheless, have not the Apostle, and Saint Thomas and Calvin himself maintained that all men, even those to whom God does not show Himself by faith, possess a rudiment of religious knowledge? Just because faith is sufficient for those who believe, we cannot validly conclude that outside faith God is in no way knowable. Certainly, we can still "forbid" those who know God by faith from seeking to know Him otherwise, and condemn all rational theology as betraying a lack of faith, or a sort of sacrilegious hesitancy about the absolute sufficiency of the divine word. That then is the last word on the question for every Calvinist who states the problem in this way; but the religious interdiction which he places on natural theology does not prevent it from still existing, even as his voluntary renunciation of a certain knowledge does not suffice to render it unknowable. The only course left open to the Calvinistic theologian is to renounce, once for all, speaking of a "philosophy" of divine things, whether it be for the purpose of reserving its use for himself, since he no longer has the right to it, or of forbidding it to others as impossible, since he, holding, as he does, grounds which make it possible, can finally deny nothing but its legitimacy.

This brings us to the fact that it is the fundamental illegitimacy of natural theology which the Calvinist is called upon to demonstrate. It is not surprising that some Calvinistic theologians, in their desire to settle the question completely, have actually gone that far. It is a decision to which Calvin himself more than once seems to have been tempted to subscribe, without, however, actually adopting it, nor was K. Barth able to do so, as far as we can see, without introducing a new shade of meaning into Calvin's thought. Certainly, when he recommends us "not to speak of the divine majesty in creation without emphasizing immediately and very strongly,[19] that, as far as we are concerned, God is *totally* hidden in nature",[20] the expression does no violence whatever to what was and always will be one of the profound exigencies of authentic Calvinism. I think it would be much more difficult to justify it on the authority of Saint Paul, for the text quoted [21] refers in fact to something quite different. Avoiding, however, the entangling brambles of exegesis, that thicket from which it is so easy to emerge with what one went looking for, it is nevertheless safe to conclude that the Barthian position does express a deeply Calvinistic view of the pauline texts. What then is its peculiar characteristic?

In order to find this out, it is necessary to recall the method always resorted to by K. Barth, in the face of the innumerable cases of this kind on which he reflects, namely, to accept simultaneously the affirmation and negation of the concrete antinomies of religious life. How, for example, ought we to speak of theology? By definition, the theologian is a *man* who ought to speak of *God;* he, who is still but a man, can only speak of God by means of God's own word: at once the grandeur and misery of theology. At one time, he is asked in the name of Saint Paul to find valid judgments on the better and the worse in a natural morality, when he knows quite well that evil reigns triumphantly in the natural moral order. Or again, he is asked to find God in His creation by the natural light, when he knows very well that all rational knowledge can no longer show "a visible order of creation" but only "a *testimony*, or a *reflection*, exclusively terrestrial, of the true order of Creation, which in our concrete circumstances remains lost and hidden for us".[22] What then must we do? Deny both terms? No, but go dialectically from one to the other and back again, assigning to each with rigorous exactitude its proper function. Since there is a moral order, there are orders of technical knowledge, of scientific knowledge, doubtless of philosophical knowledge as well, and it is precisely these which remain *reflections* exclusively terrestrial of the true order of Creation. It is important to understand that the specific character of every natural and human order is to be an order having need of *pardon*. This is its very nature and this nature is moreover the justification of the only religious function which can be attributed to it.

Let us repeat, however, that it is just such a justification. This impotence with which the dark realm of morality is stamped, is exactly what looks forward to and receives the light of pardon. Similarly, that obscurity in which rational and philosophical knowledge grows, becomes a sort of obscure background on which flashes the light of faith in the divine word. It is therefore unnecessary to treat such matters sceptically; they are questions to which God gives the answer; and if we want an answer, we have to ask the question, nor ought we to abandon them in a fit of pessimism, for, if it is true that they are only questions, God will give the answer to them. Above all, and here we reach the very depths of Barthism in these matters, we must never expect that which is a question and can never be anything else, to assume the rôle of an answer; else all is lost, even to the one meaning which alone can be attributed to such disciplines, which by their very nature are darknesses to be dissipated, miseries to be redeemed, sins to be forgiven. This explains the wish so ardently formulated by K. Barth that philosophy remain as "worldly" as possible. By which we are to understand that philosophy should confine itself within its own natural bounds, give up all religious pretensions, in short "confess itself really profane, really Godless".[23]

The tragedy of the situation is that if the secret of the world is the *non-existence* of its gods, the world itself is ignorant of it, and the Church, which alone knows it, can alone confess it for the world. The divine word, therefore, hasn't for its object the giving of God to philosophy, for it is the essence of philosophy to be without Him; nor the christianization of natural theology, for it lacks not only the desire but even the possibility of being christianized.[24] It is *because of* this impotence and as a witness to this very impotence that it is of any use; and even were we able, it would not do for us to raise it from that state. All that theology can do is to show it that it is a *negation* by placing before it, and above it, the *affirmation* of the divine word. That is why philosophy ought to be jealously confined to its proper function: namely, to attest the religious sterility, not only actual, but essential, of natural reason, and to own itself to be the permanent testimony of the definitive impotence of nature.

Such a doctrine will not be expected to undertake the redemption or rescue of philosophy by raising it to the dignity of "Christian philosophy". All the Barthian Calvinist asks of philosophy is that it recognize itself as damned and remain in that condition. Surely a hard position, and more than that, the evil is irremediable, since in no case can the certitude of God which judges philosophy (as well as ethics), become *our* certitude, and still less the certitude of philosophy. And so this discipline is finally reduced to the Lutheran position of *simul peccator et justus*. This is only what we might have expected, at least if we remembered the advice given by K. Barth to the Calvinists to begin by becoming once for all quite Lutheran.[25] That is what he himself did, but the difficulty of the position is evident from his own case, for, though be became Lutheran, he did not remain such. For, after all, in spite of the profound accord and indissoluble unity of the two Reformers, there subsists between them, besides the distance which separates the Lutheran primacy of salvation from the Calvinistic primacy of divine majesty, differences of tone which are not always negligible. The one we have just noticed is certainly not so. Philosophy, though not less completely lost in the Calvinism of Calvin than in the Lutheran-Calvinism of K. Barth, nevertheless can in the former retain some hope of salvation, and it is precisely faith which, by absorbing it, will accomplish its rescue. A decision heavy with consequences, not so much, perhaps, for philosophy itself, which, in any case, has no proper existence in its own right, but for theology. For a theology which claims from the start the title of "Christian philosophy", will never be tempted to insist extravagantly on its own misery, nor to consider itself simply as a "signal of distress".[26] In fact, the first two chapters of Calvin's *Institution* disclose a mastery and a tranquillity which allow no suspicion that any anxiety whatsoever troubled the author's mind as to the legitimacy of his work.

Such, indeed, was, as far as I can judge, the attitude of pure Calvinism, that is to say the Calvinism of Calvin himself, before it was modified by reflections from Hegel, Kirkegaard, and especially from Luther. Reduced to its essential point, it seems to me first of all to imply a total condemnation of reason, conceived as completely blind to the divine order ever since the fall. On this essential point, Lutheranism and the most authentic Calvinism agree. Thus they leave no place for a natural philosophy of divine things which would pretend to set itself up as valid. In both cases a "natural religious knowledge" appears as a monster and a contradiction in terms, which amounts to saying that all natural theology is impossible. On the other hand, authentic Calvinism seems unwilling to hurl the human intelligence once for all into total impotence, and to condemn it to that permanent misery in which K. Barth judges that it is essential to keep it. If there is no natural religious philosophy in Calvinism, there is certainly a religious certitude, and this, being the certitude of the word of God, is necessarily quite the contrary to a misery. Not that there is any question of man's sharing a partnership with God as though the Lord ought not to have all. No, the wisdom of man must perish as completely as his justice; but at least the certitude of God is immovable, and what is theology, if not the truth of God Himself, inscribed in the heart of man by the Holy Ghost? That is why Calvin so carefully attempted to construct a dogmatic theology, with contents opposed to scholastic theology and even of a different type, but of which he never doubted the intrinsic certitude, even when it transposed the postulates of natural knowledge to the plane of Revelation. Subject to the authority of the divine word, human reason is certainly no longer a philosophical reason, but it is still a reason. It is not for having used their reason, that the *Traité des scandales* reproaches Origen, Tertullian, Basil and Chrysostom, but rather for not having "used the judgment that God gave them",[27] for, to use reason to humble man completely, even opposing if necessary the most illustrious sages of the world, is still making use of it. There is then for authentic Calvinism no natural theology, not even a Christian one, and that is just where it is opposed on this point to Catholicism;[28] but at the same time it does not imply a ruthless condemnation of man to never having any "religious knowledge" properly so called, since Calvinistic theology itself claims to be such. Though it radically transcends philosophy, yet it does not disdain in case of need to adopt its title, not that it is a philosophy but because it replaces what would have been philosophy for man if sin had not blinded the light that was his, and because it consequently claims that it alone can fulfill its functions for us. In short it does not want to posit natural philosophy as possible, nor yet deliberately keep it in a state of damnation, but to transfigure it in supernatural theology, which is the only conceivable means of saving it.

If it be thus interpreted and confined within the limits of its essence, the Calvinistic position may indeed assume an exclusively theological purity (the purity, that is to say, of Calvinistic theology as such), provided that it excludes all possibility of any agreement whatever with pure rational philosophy and agrees to disappear in the measure in which it pretends to realize such an agreement. True, the facts, commented on by Saint Paul in the celebrated text which reformed dogmatic theology has never forgotten, oblige us to recognize that since God "is manifested to us in His works,

it is indeed necessary for us to seek Him in them; for our
mind is not capable of understanding His essence. And
the world is a sort of mirror for us, in which we can con-
template Him, after the manner in which it is necessary for
us to know Him".[29]   To this text may be added those of
the *Confession de la Rochelle* and of the *Confession des
Pays-Bas*, of which the second article suggests, then affirms,
a double knowledge of God, first by His creation and secondly, and in a more manifest manner,[30] by His word.
Even then it is still true to say that for the Calvinist the
knowledge of God by His creatures never assumes the least
religious value except in the light of His word. It would
only be a loss of time to call upon these theologians to explain how our purely natural knowledge of God retains any
philosophical value whatsoever; for even if it does, they are
not interested. The essence of Calvinism on this point may
be considered in a certain sense "analogous" to that of
Kantism, in this at least that it is essentially critical. Calvinism is a religious disqualification of the order of fallen
nature, as Kant's criticism was to be a scientific disqualification of the metaphysical order. Let us say, if you will, that
"religious critique" might be a suitable formula, and nothing
further, for designating that typical attitude of reformed
dogmatic theology which, in the name of a religious question first put to philosophy, completely dispossesses man of
any aptitude for approaching God by pure reason. Just as
the human will is judged "totally subject to sin", so whatever clarity our intelligence is still capable of "is converted
into darkness whenever it is a question of seeking God".
How could it be otherwise, if we begin with the principle
that man's nature is "totally corrupt"? [31] The true Calvinist
has, then, the right and the duty of letting the dead bury

what he considers to be dead. The only reason I remind him that he has no business going further is that I am convinced that a clear disagreement is often more fruitful than the vague politeness of a misunderstanding.

III

CATHOLICISM AND PHILOSOPHY

CALVINISM can seek an attitude conformable to its principles either in the suppression of one of the two terms of the antinomy or in the maintenance of the antinomy as such; Catholicism must likewise look for its true attitude, but it can only be that of an order. It is the nature of this order, therefore, that we must try to define.

But first let us note a rather disconcerting reproach levelled against the Catholic position on the problem by reformed dogmatic theology; namely, that it exalts the rights of reason to the detriment of faith or lessens the unconditional respect man owes to the majesty of the divine word. Therein is evidenced a lack of discernment, regrettable among theologians, as to the real character of the position they are attacking and from which, in the long run, neither they nor we can hope to benefit. Not only will the Calvinists never justify their own doctrine by opposing it to the pseudo-Catholicism which they criticize, but Catholics run the risk of believing themselves free from all faults simply because they are innocent of the one of which they are accused. We, however, do make mistakes. The Calvinists would render us a real service, were they to take the trouble of pointing them out to us, and I even think that their own theology would profit thereby, for we never know exactly what we do admit as long as we are mistaken about what we reject.   After all, how can we be sure that what we reject is not acceptable, if we have a mistaken conception of it?

Now in the first place, faith for the Church of Rome is not "a pure and simple intellectual adhesion to the doctrine of the infallible Church", which would indeed be opposed to the Calvinistic faith in God and His promises.[1] May one be excused here for having to cite the Act of Faith which every Catholic teaches his children from the very tenderest years; which he will repeat till his dying day, and which any Calvinistic theologian can read on the first page of our catechism?   In fact, why not recite the whole first page?   We shall see indeed if a Catholic has to learn respect for the divine majesty from Calvin.   "In the name of the Father, and of the Son, and of the Holy Ghost.   Amen. Let us place ourselves in the presence of God, let us adore His holy name.   Most holy and august Trinity, One in Three Persons, I believe that Thou art present here.   I adore Thee with sentiments of the most profound humility, and I render to Thee with my whole heart the homage which is due Thy sovereign Majesty."   It is only after this that the Act of Faith comes: "My God, I firmly believe all the truths which *Thou* hast revealed and Thou teachest us *by* Thy Church, because Thou canst neither deceive nor be deceived." [2]   I could readily understand reformed dogmatic theology reproaching us for believing God by the Church of Rome, instead of believing Him by the Confession of Rochelle or by the Confession of the reformed Walloon and Flemish Churches of the Low-Countries, later revised by the Synod of Dordrecht, or by the Confession of Augsburg, or by that of Westminster, which the Church of Scotland afterwards approved.   What surprises me is that they freely suppose that a Catholic believes less immediately in God

by the Church of Rome than a Protestant, who considers
as the faithful expression of the divine word decisions taken,
not, since that would be impious, by a *council*, but indeed
by a *synod*, assembled no matter where, provided it be not
at Rome.   When a Calvinist tells me that he refers to
La Rochelle, Embden, Dordrecht or Geneva simply because
the Church which assembled there only recorded the word
of God, the idea never strikes me that he no longer believes
in God, but in his Church.   I know full well that the only
reason why he adheres to that one Church is that, to him,
its teaching faithfully expresses the very word of God. Why,
then, does he suppose that the Catholic Church is something else for us?   Free, if he so chooses, to do battle with
imaginary foes on an illusory battlefield, we can at least let
him know that he will have to abandon all hope of ever
encountering us there.

   We can also add that, if he investigates into the actual
teaching of the Catholic faith, what he will find there has
nothing in common with "the pure and simple intellectual
adhesion" the concept of which the Reformers are supposed
to have profoundly modified.   If, as is but too certain, the
Calvinistic faith differs from the Catholic faith, it is not
because Catholic faith addresses itself first to the intellect,
for so also does that of Calvin.   Calvinistic faith is a particular gift of the Holy Ghost, rendered necessary "by the
fact that our understanding is too weak to comprehend the
spiritual wisdom of God", of such a kind that by it "the
Holy Ghost illumines and enlightens us that we may be
made capable of understanding what otherwise would be
incomprehensible to us." [3]   Nor can they differ any more
because Calvinistic faith is something besides this intellectual
adhesion, for Catholic faith is also something else.   Essen-

tially it is certainly a quality of the intellect, but not "purely and simply", since the intellect believes the divine word only because it is moved to do so by the will, as Saint Augustine said of old, which Saint Thomas interprets, by love.[4] In this sense we not only believe God (Deum) and unto God (Deo) but also in God (in Deum).[5]

There are many Catholic definitions of faith, and we could without any danger of being mistaken choose any one of the six examined in the *Summa Theologica*, but instead of fixing one up for our purposes would it not be more simple to be content with the one which Saint Thomas himself gives us as the most perfect? It is that of Saint Paul:[6] "Faith is the substance of things to be hoped for, the conviction of things that appear not." If we had to compare Saint Thomas' and Calvin's commentaries on this definition, the greater insistence on the saving power of faith would perhaps not be found on the side of the dogmatic theology of the Reformer; for if Calvin recalls that the gift of faith "*also* strengthens our confidence in God, by fixing and imprinting the promises of salvation in our hearts",[7] Saint Thomas makes of it, with Saint Paul, the very *substance*, that is to say the "first beginning" of eternal beatitude in us.[8] I will not say that the reformed definition of the Catholic faith is a caricature of it, for I know that its author had neither the intention nor the malice for that; it is merely the expression by which a Calvinistic theologian, quite spontaneously, represents that definition to himself, in order that he may more easily reject it.

If such indeed is the case, then that reproach directed against Catholicism by the dogmatic theology of the Reformer, namely, "of making the affirmation of faith rest on fallible reasonings",[9] may be placed in the same class of

arguments as those dealt with above. The affirmations of
Catholic faith ultimately depend on no reasoning, fallible
or otherwise, but on the word of God. For indeed whatever
reason is able to know about God with a perfect knowledge,
precisely because it is thus knowable, cannot essentially belong in the order of faith. It can happen that most men
have to believe such things: that is the case with all those
who cannot or do not desire to know them; but no matter
how often that occurs, it is merely accidental and does not
suffice for the incorporation *de jure* of these truths into the
body of faith. They are only preambles of it; precisely
because they are, of themselves, accessible to reason. God
exists, He is One, the Creator of the world, Intelligent and
Willing, Wise and Provident: these are indeed certitudes
necessary for salvation (and God has revealed them); but
since they remain of themselves naturally knowable, they
bear to proper beliefs the same relationship as nature bears
to grace. Not so with the body of those truths which are
essentially of faith; for even when reasoning intervenes
there, the value of its conclusions rests entirely on the certitude of the divine word and not inversely.

Let a man, then, mistrust the power of his reason, his
faith will nevertheless have nothing to fear. What is in
itself knowable about God, and yet he does not know, he
can at least believe. No man entertained fewer illusions
than Saint Thomas about the general ability of men for understanding metaphysics. After all, he was a professor; so he
had pupils of his own to teach. All that Calvin has been
credited with having *already* remarked concerning the weakness of natural reason and the dangers which accompany the
very delicate handling of metaphysical reasonings repro-
duces, purely and simply, the classic text of the *Summa*

Contra Gentiles,[10] and many another in which Saint Thomas enumerates the reasons why it is fitting that God has prescribed that all men hold by faith all the salutary truths, so that all may share in them without doubt or error. There is, in Catholic theology, a very important, though anonymous, person, whose existence ought never to be forgotten by those wishing to criticize it deliberately. It is the "old woman". The *vetula* of our theologians doesn't know a word of philosophy, and it is precisely for that reason that they admire her, to such an extent that we sometimes wonder if they don't even envy her a little. Thus Saint Bonaventure, recalling the lesson of Brother Giles (a *simplex et ydiota* like Saint Francis himself) says, "the fact is that an old woman, with a little garden, but who possesses charity, derives more fruit from it alone than a great master with an extensive garden and a knowledge of the mysteries of nature".[11]

But are we, as a matter of fact, even certain that he does know these mysteries of nature? St. Thomas himself had his doubts: "Our knowledge is so weak, that no philosopher has ever been able to know perfectly the nature of a fly; that is why, we read, a philosopher spent thirty years in solitude in order to know the nature of the bee". If, then, our intellect is so weak, is it not foolish to want to believe of God only those things which man by himself can know of Him? That is just what is condemned in Job: "Behold God is great, exceeding our knowledge". [12] Such, therefore, is for a Catholic theologian the sum total of the accounts of so many centuries of natural theology: "No philosopher before the advent of Christ, devoting all his energy to it, was able to know as much about God and what is necessary for eternal life, as a poor woman knows about these things by faith

since the advent of Christ".[13]   Instructed by this time-hon-
oured experience, the true Catholic, most enamoured of philosophy, hardly has the illusion of knowing perfectly what,
of itself, is perfectly knowable.   Not only is he more certain
of what he believes than of what he knows, but he believes
quae sunt fidei magis quam ea quae videt: what he believes
is more certain for him than what he sees.

For anyone remembering what exactly is the essential
order of faith in authentic Catholicism, and that it admits
only one single perfect knowledge: "Christ the power of
God and the wisdom of God, who of God is made unto us
wisdom",[14] the accusation directed against our theologians, of pretending to find truth by reason alone, but actually allowing themselves to be unconsciously directed by
faith,[15] appears truly amazing.   How would a Catholic
theologian allow himself to be "unconsciously" led by a
faith which he openly holds as the very principle of his research?   All that is necessary is to reply with Saint Thomas:
"*Contra, Hebr.* xi, 6: *sine fide impossibile est placere Deo.*
But to please God is supremely necessary.   Since, then, philosophy is powerless with regard to anything which depends
on faith, there must be another knowledge which proceeds
from the principles of faith".[16]   That is why the Vatican
Council declares in fitting terms that the science of faith
revealed by God "is not proposed to the ingenuity of men
as a philosophic invention to be perfected, but as a divine
deposit, entrusted to the Spouse of Christ, to be faithfully
guarded and infallibly interpreted."   In no case does the
theologian, as such, try to pretend to find by reason alone
what is taught by faith.   As theologian, he speaks in the
name of God, and that is sufficient.   If he proves rationally
what is capable of being naturally known, the theologian is

only making use of philosophy for the moment and speaks as a philosopher. The essential order of faith, that is, things which can be believed only, is not involved here at all; but what is more, even in such cases the theologian, far from allowing himself to be unconsciously guided by Revelation in the use he makes of natural reason, actually keeps his eyes fixed on it as on the surest of guides. He doesn't deduce anything from it here nor prove anything by it, but he relies on the word of God to deliver his reason from error, protect it and instruct it.[17] All that the theologian wishes to do is to prove to those who are capable of it, that what God has here prescribed for them to believe, they can know. What attitude could be more conscious? To guide his reason along the path traced by Revelation without being conscious of it, would be to take a star for a guide without perceiving it.

At this point, however, it were well for us Catholics as well as the Calvinists to make an examination of conscience. When the Calvinist has proclaimed himself irremediably corrupted, he runs the risk of resigning himself quite comfortably to his corruption; when the Catholic has professed his hope in healing grace, it is to be feared that he may believe himself so well healed that he may soon want to do without grace. In both cases original sin comes into its own again. The point is not without application in the present discussion. If reformed dogmatic theology believes itself authorized in criticizing what it calls Catholic rationalism, it is perhaps because certain Catholics express themselves as though the science of the preambles of faith, namely, natural theology, under the pretext that it is essentially rational, were a religiously neutral domain, wherein Revelation exercises no positive and direct influence. I don't think it is possible for a Catholic to maintain that without forgetting certain essential facts which must be kept in mind.

When a Catholic theologian maintains that, among the truths necessary to salvation and revealed by God, some are accessible to reason alone, such as the existence of one God, the sole Creator of the world, he does not only speak of a *de jure* possibility, but also of a *de facto* possibility. It remains to be seen, nevertheless, in what proportion and under what conditions it is realizable. If experience proves that this natural knowledge of God, certain though limited in profundity, is possible, it also shows how difficult it is in practice to attain it when reason is left completely to itself. We could not wish for more convincing experience in this regard than the results obtained by the most profound human minds, as long as they had to speak of God without being guided by Revelation. How can we but conclude that, as Saint Thomas has remarked, in these matters "our researches easily lead us into error because of the weakness of our intellect. This is clearly shown by the example of the philosophers who, looking for the end of human life by following the path of reason, and failing to discover the way of attaining it, fell into so many and such abominable errors, contradicting one another so much that we can scarcely find two or three holding one opinion identical on every point in these matters, whereas we see even several peoples agree in the same opinion by faith." [18]

Our next step is to determine whether the fact that successes of this kind were extremely rare of old compels us to conclude that they ought necessarily to be the same today. Why would not the universality of faith be reflected in a sort of universality of philosophical reason? We are no longer in the same situation as Plato and Aristotle, first, be-

cause though possessing less genius we benefit by the progress due to them; but even more because a divine aid is now
available which was lacking to them. Since God Himself
has revealed His existence, every man has to begin by believing it, even though he be a future Plato or Aristotle.
Before the day when the child will have become an illustrious metaphysician, it will be necessary, supposing that he
is able to do it, to leave him time for learning almost all the
other sciences, necessary preambles of metaphysics, though
few indeed comprehend or attain them all (*"quae quidem
praeambula paucissimi comprehendunt vel consequuntur"*).
Meanwhile who will teach him God? In the beginning, our
intellect is empty; we need, however, to know God immediately, "and that is why our intellect at the risk of being at
any time without the knowledge of God, has need of faith
that by it, it may receive the divine truths from the very
beginning." It is, therefore, also true that a Christian man
ought to believe those things which he could by rights understand about God without ever having believed them.[19]
(That is why Saint Thomas does not apply to this order of
truths the *nisi credideritis non intelligetis*). No wonder
then if Christians, with greater facility than the pagans, discover by their reason those things which they almost always
begin by believing.

It is not then without some reason that a Calvinistic
theologian was recently astonished to see a Catholic philosopher pass on the question this judgment which seems to deny
purely and simply the possibility of a Catholic believing
in the existence of God: "Revelation is *morally* necessary to
humanity in order to conserve its patrimony of speculative
and moral truths. It is not *physically* necessary to it; and,
in any case, the existence of God cannot be made the object

of an act of divine faith." [20]   That Revelation is only
morally necessary to safeguard the essential postulates of
natural theology, we quite agree, but this principle does not
justify the remark which accompanies it.   The existence of
God can be known without being believed, but it can be believed without being known by philosophical knowledge and
with an unshakable metaphysical certitude.   Such is precisely the reason why Saint Thomas Aquinas was just reminding us that our intellect has need of faith "that by it it may
receive the divine truths from the very beginning".   Furthermore when a grown man does not feel able to grasp
the cogency of metaphysical demonstrations, he has to believe on the faith of the divine word that God exists.   Now
how could he believe in God on the faith of God without
believing in Him by an act of divine faith?   We understand,
then, how a Calvinistic theologian, reading such a formula,
might allow himself to be deceived, but it really falls short
of correctly expressing the Catholic position on this point.

In fact, the very reality of faith is too rich and the
variety of human experiences is too great for a single formula to be able to define anything but *de jure* truth.   If we
consider what happens *de facto*, it will no longer suffice to
distinguish those who believe from those who know.   Another class, of no small number, will have to be taken into
account, namely, those who do nothing but believe, though
they flatter themselves with knowing.   For after all, what
is a necessary proof for Saint Augustine is not so for Saint
Thomas Aquinas, and what is so for Saint Thomas Aquinas is
not so for Duns Scotus.   I am willing to admit that one of
them is right, but then the others must be mistaken.   Let
us take a concrete example, and one too that is well known.
Saint Anselm was absolutely certain of having given an evi-

dent, irrefutable and even unshakable proof of the existence of God in his *Proslogium*. Having attained his conclusion, he declared himself so sure of it that, said he, even if he no longer believed in the existence of God, it would have henceforth been impossible for him not to know it. If he knew it, it was no longer at all because he believed it, and the faith which he kept of it was irrelevant to the knowledge he had acquired of it. Everyone knows, nevertheless, that in the eyes of Saint Thomas this pretended rational evidence was only a *petitio principii*. In so far as his scientific certitude of the existence of God rested on this argument, it was then nothing more than faith in the guise of a proof, and what was the case of Saint Anselm will be that also of Descartes and of Malebranche. Descartes would have been quite surprised if someone told him his proof of the existence of God, which he considered just as certain or even more certain than any mathematical demonstration whatever, was only the metaphysical formula of the most simple act of faith; for judged from the Thomistic point of view it was in the most *favorable hypothesis* nothing else; for is it not at least possible that because certain men have played with proofs for the existence of God they have come to find themselves in the position where they neither knew, nor believed it, with consequences that we may guess, though we cannot go into them here? False proofs do not germinate in the souls of fathers, because they still believe; but when the sons perceive that they are false, it is too late, for they themselves no longer believe. Having been taught that God's existence is not a matter of faith, they themselves are left without either belief or proof. It is thus that from a Descartes a Voltaire can be born, and from a Malebranche a Hume. In treating these concrete questions with the detached disinterestedness of the abstract philosopher, we forget the rights of the psychologist, of the moralist and consequently also of the theologian.

Concerning this, Saint Thomas himself has made a remark in a form which though quite simple is none the less valuable: it is a common mistake for a man to think something is proven which is not *(frequenter in hoc homo fallitur, quod putat esse demonstrationem quod non est)*.[21] I confess that, as far as I am concerned, this prudent statement is sufficient to make me recoil before the intrepid assurance of those who say that "man can be obliged to admit God only if he *demonstrates* His existence; the worship that he renders Him can be meritorious only if it is reasonably and convincingly established."[22] No! Man is obliged to admit God on the sole authority of the divine word, even though he believes himself incapable of demonstrating His existence; and not only is the worship which he renders to God meritorious in the absence of a complete intellectual conviction, but perhaps it is never more so than in the case when a man persists in rendering it in the midst of the darkness of a wavering reason, as a blind man whose hands alone assure him of the presence of the altar.

The truth of the matter is perhaps that a problem as complex as the one for which we are seeking an answer is not susceptible of a simple solution valid for every case. The first of the preambles of faith is the affirmation of the existence of God. Of itself, it is a truth naturally knowable without the light of faith. That is indeed why, according to the words of St. Paul, those who deny it are inexcusable. It is therefore certain that human reason, however weakened and darkened by original sin, conserves enough strength to guide it with certitude to the existence of God. But this natural knowledge of God by reason is not always, in fact, the absolute certitude that it might be. It can happen, as Saint Thomas says, that it be a weak estimation *(debilis existimatio)* of reason. Things therefore are going to take a rather complicated course. The man who begins by deeming, without being very sure of it, that God exists, can come to the further estimation that it ought to be pleasing to God that we believe Him, and especially that we believe that He exists. And so, very far from thinking that the natural knowledge that we have of God excludes necessarily faith in His existence, Saint Thomas expressly teaches that this spontaneous inference which posits God beginning with the order of the world, the moral aspirations of man or the problem of his destiny, invites us to believe that God exists. *Et sic potest aliquis credere Deum esse, eo quod sit placitum Deo;* not, adds St. Thomas, that the existence of God is an article of faith, since it is demonstrable, but it is here believed by an act of faith, which is midway between the rational estimation which is a preparation for it and a scientific demonstration, the realization of which, though always possible, is yet unforeseen.[23] Not only, then, is faith in the existence of God not impossible, but we see it in this instance called upon to reinforce an opinion which does not feel sure of itself and which, while waiting for the demonstration lacking to it, has no other complete assurance than that of faith.

It can happen that for want of means or leisure reason never attempts this scientific and technical demonstration. Such, it seems, is the case of a great number of men, that their reason tends rather towards faith in the existence of God than towards the technical demonstration of this truth. These, evidently, will be very far from getting along without faith, since, on the contrary, it is their reason itself which calls for it. As for those who will attempt to go beyond their *debilis existimatio* of the existence of God in order to raise themselves to the scientific proof of this truth, it may happen that they succeed, in which case the existence of God will become for them, what it is in itself: a demonstratively proven certitude which precedes the body of the truths of faith; but it can also happen that they fail, in which case it is desirable that faith be there to assist the spontaneous inferences of reason in surviving the eventual shipwreck of their demonstration! The fool who says in his heart: there is no God, is much less often a simpleton, docile to the inspirations of natural reason, than an imperfect philosopher, who wants reason to provide that which, without the efforts and the intellectual and moral preparations necessary, it cannot give him.

Are we then going to maintain that there may not be under the act of faith in the existence of God this valid rational inference which man, even outside Revelation, would be inexcusable for not making? Or would we maintain inversely that every man is strictly bound by this inference to seek technically demonstrative proofs which will dispense him from faith? Never, it seems to me, has the Church taught such a doctrine. God is not reserved for professors or students of philosophy, and Saint Thomas certainly never wished anything of the sort. It is true to say in good Thomistic doctrine that the same truth cannot be believed and known, at one time and under the same aspect. What a man knows about God, that is to say, what he knows by a scientifically valid proof, he could not therefore at the same time believe. That simply proves that a natural theology is *possible* and that, whenever it is truly realized, it dispenses

from faith. But it in no way proves that a validly demonstrated natural theology is a necessary condition of human
salvation, nor that a worship which is not based on it must
be considered as of no religious value, nor, finally and above
all, that faith in the existence of God is so useless that we
may with impunity hold it to be impossible.

Revelation contains every salutary truth, not only those
which are essentially of faith and will always remain so, but
even those preambles which, of themselves knowable, can
nevertheless not be immediately known by anyone, and will
perhaps never be known by some. So far from the act of
faith in these preliminary truths being impossible, God has
expressly revealed them in order that they may be believed.
That is why, says Saint Thomas, it was necessary "for us to
know from the beginning by faith those things which our
reason was still unable to attain, *et hoc quantum ad ea quae
ad fidem praeexiguntur*".[24] And it is not just a question of
an abstract possibility but of a practical and concrete necessity. We can here say with Kant: "You ought, therefore
you can"; for not only has God permitted us to believe even
the comprehensible, He has prescribed it for us: "salubriter
ergo divina providit clementia, *ut ea etiam quae ratio inves-
tigare potest*, fide tenenda *praeciperet*".[25] It is therefore not
only possible to believe in the existence of but one God, but
it can even be necessary: *necesse est credere Deum esse
unum, et incorporeum, quae naturali ratione a philosophis
probantur*, and that is necessary, as Saint Thomas expressly
says, for certitude *(propter certitudinem)*, because human
reason is very deficient in things pertaining to God *(ratio
humana in rebus divinis est multum deficiens)*.[26] In short,
faith does not deal only with what is essentially of faith, it
extends to everything that may be revealed, that is to say

to anything which God judges opportune to reveal. In this sense, the preambles of faith themselves, though they can be proven, can also be believed: *possunt demonstrari et sciri.* Such is, in particular, the case of the existence of God: *sicut hoc quod est Deum esse,* this truth being believed by anyone whose intellect has not attained the demonstration of it, for faith suffices by itself to firmly assure us of everything which precedes it as well as of everything which follows it.[27] When we disclose too much eagerness in keeping theology separated from philosophy, we are liable to forget the most elementary principles of theology.

It is not surprising that those who no longer even think that a Catholic can believe in the existence of God on the faith alone of the divine word, refuse to admit that natural theology can owe anything to the positive teachings of Revelation. What we have never believed in evidently owes nothing to faith when it is known; but the simple Christian who believes in God, and that He is One, and the Father Almighty, Creator of heaven and of earth, cannot be prevented from thinking that what he believes, if it is possible also to know it, is taught to him that he may both believe and know it. Doubtless, taken in itself, the reason of the Christian differs in no way from that of the pagan. It is a reason. No special illumination, no grace created anew, comes to unveil for it the philosophical conclusions, knowledge of which would be reserved to it. Created and conserved by God as a natural light, moved by Him in the presence of this sensible nature, where His Providence is manifested by His works, the Christian's reason can know Him, even as any other reason, without further help *(sine novi luminis infusione),* in the measure at least in which He is naturally knowable to reason.[28] Nevertheless, the reason

CATHOLICISM AND PHILOSOPHY

of the Christian, though formally identical with that of the pagan, is placed in a different situation than the latter, because it is the reason of a man endowed with grace. We can refuse, as philosophers, to take account of this situation and be satisfied with observing that the act required "to attain a truth till then unknown is *in itself* the same as the act by which a truth already known is proven", but though observation proves indeed that a reason which knows with faith ought to be capable of knowing without faith, and so opposes the semi-traditionalism which is in fact untenable, it does not authorize us to maintain that, the operation being intrinsically the same in both cases, the revelation of what we can comprehend only diminishes the *extrinsic* difficulties, which beset our proving it.[29]

That is in fact an arbitrary simplification of a very complex situation, the nature of which the philosopher can, strictly speaking, be unaware, but about which no Catholic theologian could possibly be deceived. Metaphysical speculation is not easy for anyone and it is a commonplace that this last of the sciences is also the most difficult of all; but the difficulties which the natural reason runs up against, when it is at grips with problems of this order, are surely intrinsic to these problems, and the greater or less trouble with which reason finds its way there does not seem less intrinsic to reason. If the divine word obtains a hearing and solves in advance for the reason a certain number of the problems with which it struggles, shall we say that, on account of coming from without, this word does not penetrate within, is not accepted there, and by telling a reason not yet sure of it: this is true, it does not make it any easier for it to see why it is true? The arguments which militate against semi-traditionalism, according to which a purely rational demonstration of the existence of God is impossible, here turn on what might be called semi-rationalism, according to which, in order for such a demonstration to be purely rational, it is necessary that the assistance offered by Revelation act only on what is extrinsic to reason. It is admitted here, in fact, by hypothesis, that what the word of God introduces into reason is naturally knowable; how, then, will we maintain that this intelligible, thus placed by God in a reason which is looking for it, does not act on it as a light? Does giving the answer to a problem only take away the extrinsic difficulties, which confuse the discussion of it? Certainly, the solution still remains to be found, but the reason striving for it, though it remains intrinsically the same, finds itself in a situation intrinsically different, since it at least knows what it is that it is trying to demonstrate. Just as, therefore, Revelation could not make reason capable of proving God if it were essentially incapable of doing so, so also, what it reveals will not be truly rationally knowable if its action remains extrinsic to reason.

Here, perhaps, more than anywhere else in this discussion, the collective efforts of competent theologians for seeking a solution are to be desired, for many questions still arise as to the specific nature of the knowledge which Revelation gives to man of truths that are naturally knowable. Doubtless, it is first of all necessary to distinguish between Revelation known without the assent of faith, and with that assent. It is perhaps also fitting to distinguish between knowledge of the existence of God as a fact, attested by Revelation and accepted by faith, and the philosophical knowledge of His existence as a truth acquired by the intelligence. I wonder if it would not even be compatible with the doctrine of Saint Thomas to say that in a sense the existence of God as known by us is not identical with His existence as believed by us. After all the Christian says: *Credo in Deum*, that is to say that, until his dying day, philosopher or not, he continues to believe *in Deum* in the theological and technical sense of the formula. Is it possible that a person can believe *in Deum*, without believing *Deo* and without believing *Deum?* That is a problem. In any case, since the philosophical knowledge of God can in no wise dispense from faith *in Deum*, it must then coexist with this faith. That is not impossible in good Thomistic doctrine, since faith and knowledge, even taking them in the limited field of the simple preambles of faith with which we are here concerned (the existence of God, unicity of God, etc.) would indeed be *de eodem*, but not *secundum idem*. We see at least what simplification a theologian like P. Geiger, O.P., can permit himself when he thinks he is setting down the question in a formula as summary as the following: "As soon as faith intervenes in the name of an assent given to any truth whatever, the domain of philosophy ceases".[30] Thus in order to be a philosopher, a Christian would calmly cease to believe in the existence of God, One, Wise, Creator, etc. I would like to know at what moment Saint Thomas thought himself authorized in amputating the very beginning of the Apostles' creed? Actually, for him, to believe in God is to believe that He, Who can be known, or indeed Whose existence and attributes are known, is also He of Whom everything else can only be believed. There is then a way of attaining the existence of God by faith from which no demonstration can dispense, since this background of mystery is in continuity with our act of faith in the existence of God, in an essentially different way than it can be with our knowledge of His existence.[31] To believe that God exists, is *credere Deum esse sub his conditionibus quas fides determinat;* those who pretend to believe otherwise, *non vere Deum credunt;* but one never *knows* His existence under the conditions determined by faith, since a great part of them remain strictly unknowable to us. We must then believe that the God whose existence we rationally know is the very same God of whom we believe what we cannot know. There is reason, consequently, for wondering if the rational knowledge of the existence of God, though it deals with the same God, can do away with the simple act of faith, which embraces at one sweep all that we can know of God and all that we have to believe of Him; since a deficiency in the cognition of simple things is simply not to attain them at all *(quia in simplicibus defectus cognitionis est solum in non attingendo totaliter).*[32] Briefly, and likewise, it seems to me, respecting common experience, when the philosopher believes, he does not have to begin his faith where his philosophical experiences leave off; and it is God in His entirety, of whom his belief includes everything together, to whom he prays, and not that part which he can only believe. I hope the theologians will be willing to accept the reflections here proposed to them as subject to their judgment.

To get rid of these supreme difficulties, it would without doubt suffice simply to return to the traditional position of the Church, and in no way diminish faith, either in its dignity or in its efficacy. The Vatican Council decrees that reason can know with certitude the preambles and foundations of faith, but it has never, it seems to me, denied that faith itself can or even ought to aid reason in its effort to know them. It has indeed expressly stated the contrary, since it affirms that the aid which faith and reason bring each other is a *mutual* aid. In this exchange, right reason dem-

CATHOLICISM AND PHILOSOPHY

onstrates the foundations of faith; it can therefore do it only if it is right; and why is it right? Because, in return, faith "frees reason from errors, protects it and provides it with many a notion".[33] In order to simplify the problem, let us be satisfied with the first of these services: is the freeing of it from its errors merely the clearing away of obstacles extrinsic to reason? The teaching of the Council, when taken as it stands, is, then, at once precise and simple, for it only summarizes the constant practice of the Doctors of the Church by saying, with regard to this matter, that faith efficaciously assists reason to get along without faith wherever that is possible, that it "assists and makes" the human sciences "progress" in many ways, so that they, coming from God, are capable, *juvante ejus gratia,* of leading us back to Him.

These considerations have more than a theological bearing, at a time when a free and easy access to the proofs of the existence of God is supposed to be opened to all Catholics. The attempt is in itself quite comprehensible, and in a sense, inevitable, granted the age in which we live. If the Church does not teach its own metaphysics to the whole world, the State will be alone in teaching *its* metaphysics; aided by book, press and even posters, which provoke the people to public debates on these matters, it will have all the more chance of getting its doctrine accepted, the more it follows the easy natural path of original sin. That is perhaps no reason for us to be satisfied with doing exactly the opposite, which is often the worst sort of imitation. Here is a battle in which we ought to take part, but we are beaten before we start if we agree to fight as do our adversaries. To do so is to eliminate or suppress from our method of philosophizing everything which, by rendering it Christian, can help in rendering it true.

There is reason, therefore, first of all for reminding those who demand metaphysical instruction from the Church, that intellectual modesty is a great virtue and that the first condition, for anyone wishing to approach God by the intelligence, is never to forget that if the intelligence fails us, our faith at least should never do so. Perhaps we might even recall that those only who are qualified for the task ought to attack problems of this kind and that we have no more right to require our first curate to prove to us in five minutes the existence of God by demonstrative reason than to require Einstein to prove his system to anyone at all in twenty-four hours. That is not, I am afraid, what we do. It seems to me, on the contrary, that, allowing ourselves to be carried away on the sea of intellectual democracy, we accept the challenge flung down by the world, to demonstrate anything at all to anyone at all. The world will fail and will pay, in temporal suffering, the expense of its temporal experience. We shall also fail if in the least we attempt to do the same thing; but since our attempt shall have been in the spiritual, it is also the spiritual that will suffer from it.

Is it not possible that our pulpits might preach a little less technical philosophy and a little more of the Gospel? I refer here especially to that sort of philosophic inflation which authorizes the dialectical proving of the existence of God, by the first mover, or by the contingent and the necessary, to the faithful assembled for the eleven o'clock Mass? However cultivated and intelligent we may suppose them to be, they are not an audience of metaphysicians. I admit there has been a general progress in knowledge, but what progress would have had to be made in order that we should reach that stage, when we recall that in the golden age of theology Saint Thomas found only the *paucissimi* to have the leisure, the desire, the intelligence and the knowledge required by anyone who wished to rise to the level of metaphysics! Having himself to speak one day before the masters and students of the University of Paris on the Apostles' Creed, the Angelic Doctor did not judge it expedient to preach to them technical and complicated proofs of the existence of God. If this select audience did not inspire him with more confidence, would it not be wise to use the same prudence with common men, and tell them: "The first thing that we have to believe is that there is One God only; the second is that this God is the Creator of heaven and earth. And in order for the present to leave aside subtle reasons, we shall make use of a crude example to show that everything was made and created by God". We may be sure that what follows, for it is really only the proof from the degrees of perfection, was indeed for Saint Thomas a proof, but, accompanied by an act of faith, it was chosen and formulated as simply as possible. The illustrious theologian, when preaching, appealed to that universal and spontaneous notion of God which is unincumbered by demonstration, rather than to any scientific discussions made for specialists. Many minds, capable of appreciating the certitude of a simple rational proof, lose sight of it in the maze of its demonstration.

This philosophical discretion might still be imitated fruitfully. Let us remember then, that for the ordinary man there is no difference between a proof which is not conclusive and a proof which he is unable to see is conclusive. No man can be made responsible for not understanding

what God simply asks him to believe, if he is unable or unwilling to make the effort necessary for achieving its understanding.   When, therefore, the objection is put to us that
today everybody wants proofs, the reply can only be that
today technical proofs are accessible to everybody.   Today
as in the 13th century, technical proofs are good for those
who can understand them; to those who cannot do so, it is
good simply to recall the old saying of Hesiod, cited by
Aristotle and commented on by Saint Thomas: "The excellent
pupil is one who can learn all alone; the good pupil is one
who can learn from others; as for him who can learn neither
alone nor from others, he is not made for science."   Neglecting any other moral, this lesson ought to inspire in us at
least some notion of what the knowing of anything really
is, which wouldn't be exactly useless for those pretending to
demonstrate the existence of God.   To engage in natural
theology all those who wish it and yet lack the necessary
preparations is to replace faith for all by science for all in
those matters in which the voice of God makes itself heard
simply because science in them is reserved to some.

That an attempt be made to generalize such a science
prudently and without grave danger, it would not even
suffice that all the human conditions of time, leisure, personal effort and intellectual aptitude be realized.   If what
we have said is true, faith would still be necessary.   By that
I do not at all mean that we must hold the existence of God
as demonstrable only for those who believe it; I have even
expressly remarked that for a Catholic, and more particularly for a Thomist, the possibility of proving God by reason
alone, in the absence of all Revelation, is a fact of experience.   I merely say that this fact does not authorize us in
neglecting Revelation once it has been given to us, and that

if we are right in thinking that the agreement of reasons with regard to the divine nature, exceptional in pagan times, ought to be much more frequent in Christian times, it is only because the reason of a Christian man is not in the same state as that of a pagan man. The only hope of success, if we wish to diffuse the teaching of natural theology as much as possible, is then to maintain more firmly than ever its real connections with revealed theology, instead of striving to weaken them. In the absence of other reasons, two considerations ought to convince us of this necessity.

First, it cannot be mere coincidence that the great masters of our natural theology are found to be at the same time the great masters of revealed theology. The middle ages have already attempted the experiment of a separated philosophy, and the result was Averroism. Every time those who wanted to teach the rational truth about God were not at the same time those who taught the Word of God, the divorce was not slow in appearing. The One, True God, Creator and Lord, of whom the Vatican Council affirms that natural reason can know with certitude, is the God of Abraham, Isaac and Jacob, become, thanks to the light of Revelation, the God of philosophers and savants. For all those who wish to find Him in their turn by reason, the wisest thing is to seek Him in the same way. Besides, it is not doubtless any more of a coincidence, that what natural reason may know with certitude, many a natural reason does not so know, or even doubts, when it doesn't go so far as to deny it. For it is no longer a question here of ignorance, or lack of leisure, or intellectual inaptitude. The professionals of scientific or philosophical thought, whose natural reason denies God in the name of the principles of reason, ought to be naturally capable of perceiving the compulsive

force of proofs such as those which Saint Thomas uses in his
Summa Theologica. They are given five ways of going to
God; they refuse them all, and yet we know that reason
alone can know God with certitude. Why does theirs not
know Him? Why, to put it bluntly, is the philosophic
world divided into two groups: those who have proofs of the
existence of a transcendent being and who believe in Him,
and those who, not believing in Him, judge such proofs to
be impossible? To put the same question rather rudely, for
which I beg to be excused: Why is the philosophy called
Scholastic true only for Catholics, taught, when it is taught,
only by Catholics, and absent, because unknown, misunder-
stood or denied, wherever Catholicism is absent? Experience, to be sure, suffers some exceptions, the number of
which I do not know, but it is quite sufficiently general to
give one pause. "For me," said P. Peillaube one day to the
philosopher G. Séailles, from whom I got the anecdote, "being
is the plenitude." "For me," replied Séailles, "it is the void."
It seems, however, that being is the proper object of our intellect; how then explain the fact that so many even philosophical intellects are incapable of seeing it? The old
theological argument, "by the contradictions of the philosophers", is not without its lesson for the philosopher himself,
which is that reason can hope for a relative unity which will
save it from disorder, only when the perfect unity of faith is
reflected in it.

That such a conclusion may not remain sterile it must
be taken frankly in its full meaning. The philosophical
unity towards which we are striving could not be a simple
verbal agreement on some formulae, nor could it consist in
a simple extension of that to include a mutual understanding
not to think certain things, but indeed to think in unison

other things.   It is not sufficient, therefore, merely to admit, as some would like, that faith play the rôle of a purely *negative* norm for philosophical speculation, only reminding it of what it has no right to think.   If we were to subscribe to that attitude, we would be far removed from appreciating the divine gift of faith at its full value.   Placed by God at the disposition of all for their salvation, it teaches philosophers not only those things of which they have no right to think the contrary, but indeed those which they ought to admit like everybody else, and consequently, also, those which they ought to think, in the measure in which they do think.   What faith prescribes for the philosopher, in the order of natural theology with which we are here concerned, is, therefore, first of all, to think what he, like everyone else, is bound to believe.   When Scripture teaches that there is a God, Who is One, True, Creator and Lord of all things, Intelligent, Wise, Free and Just, it not only does something more than, but also something quite different from, merely placing barriers outside which reason cannot venture without being certain of erring.   It teaches positive truths, rich with rational content, apt, consequently, to become scientific certitudes for an intellect capable of understanding them. It not only forbids anyone from attempting to prove the contrary, but also commands him to prove what it has revealed, if at least he wants to prove anything at all in these matters, or else be satisfied with believing it, if he doesn't know how to prove it.   Either to demonstrate the preambles of faith, and know them, or not to demonstrate them, and believe them, we have no other choice.

To go thus far, and that deliberately, it is useful to remember that no conception of philosophy can be acceptable from the Catholic point of view (and it ought to be the same even for those Catholics who reject the notion of Christian philosophy), unless the conception of nature to which it is joined be itself Catholic. The first thing to find out, therefore, is whether our nature, wounded by original sin, can wisely neglect the remedy supplied by God Himself for its wound. Saint Thomas constantly justifies the necessity of Revelation by the weakness of human reason which, left to itself, would inevitably become entangled in the grossest errors. Since when is the human reason so weak? When St. Thomas enumerates the wounds inflicted on human nature by the sin of Adam, he never forgets to mention ignorance, by which reason is stripped of its disposition for truth.[34] We could not of ourselves remedy this loss suffered by our natural reason. To be sure, the very essence of human reason was left intact and even the natural aptitude of man to know the truth has suffered less from original sin than his aptitude to will the good;[35] but nevertheless, because our reason is the knowing power of a human nature wounded by sin, it did suffer from it, and it still suffers from each supplementary wound that new sins inflict on it. We have therefore come back to that fundamental Catholic postulate, namely, that fallen nature, although it can do something, can, however, no longer do all the good connatural to it so that it never fail in any way *(totum bonum sibi connaturale ita quod in nullo deficiat)*.[36] Man, remarks St. Thomas, can still build houses and plant vineyards, though perhaps not so well as before. Let us concede without further ado that he can also construct a philosophy and even that he remains more capable of thinking well than of doing well;[37] but the detriment suffered by his nature remains and only a divine intervention can remove it. Faith in the divine Word brings this grace to us, and to accept it is to philosophize as a Christian. To forget what good remains in nature is fatal to Catholicism, but to forget what nature has suffered and the remedies which its weakness calls for would be none the less fatal to it. The truly Catholic attitude, in face of the philosophical tasks which confront us, consists, therefore, in never despairing of reason, but in carefully availing ourselves of the supernatural aids that God offers the reason, in order to permit the same to succeed in its enterprises. The hope remains for us that one day the knowledge of the truth will completely replace in us a faith thenceforth useless, but that will be the day which has no end. For the pilgrims that we are, it is hardly probable that natural theology can set itself up as the "preamble of faith" without taking account of the faith of which it desires to be the preamble. Rather indeed is it necessary to ask that faith diligently to preserve for us all the essential postulates of this science in order to lead our reason towards them, or to restore them to it if we happen to lose them. In short, let this science be ours, but let us not say that we owe it only to ourselves. He who wishes to think truly as a Catholic will do well never to forget the great saying of Saint Paul to the Ephesians: "that henceforward you walk not as also the Gentiles walk in the vanity of their mind: having their understanding darkened".[38] Saint Thomas applies this text, which he himself quotes in his *Summa Contra Gentiles*,[39] precisely to the truths naturally knowable to man. A Catholic natural theology is therefore possible for the intellect assisted by the divine Word which dispels the darkness and shields it from vanity.

IV

THEOLOGY AND PHILOSOPHY

ONCE the foregoing considerations have been established, the problem of the relation between theology and philosophy demands a solution, and that with imperative necessity. Such, of course, is not the opinion of K. Barth, and the reason is not hard to understand. "Is there anything more pitiful", he asks, "than the attempt developed through the ages, to determine a systematic connection or, inversely, a systematic distinction between the domains of theology and of philosophy? Is there to be found a single philosopher worthy of that name who pays the least attention to the ingenuous constructions of theologians devoted to that task? Would not the anxiety, the uncertainty with which they devote themselves to it, make it apparent that this task can only have been undertaken with a bad conscience? It is evident that theology can become interesting for philosophy only when it forgoes all effort to interest it." [1] Perhaps, but it is just then that theology becomes supremely interesting to the philosopher. That no one of importance among them is ever interested in the problem of the borderline between theology and philosophy, such as theologians posit it, simply goes to prove (supposing the fact itself is true) that philosophy is much nearer confessing its secret than we are told. But if you want theology to make it confess, it is obvious that theology is strictly obliged to state the problem. That is what Catholic theology does. The hesitation, the prudent lengths it observes in giving an answer to it, are not signs of a bad conscience, but the proof that it has a conscience. It is always easier to cut off a member than to cure it; but as long as its incurability is not absolutely certain, to cut it off is a heavy responsibility.

A statement of the question such as that to which the Catholic finds himself led is of its very nature complex, since he must always take into account two elements: reason which for him cannot have become totally incapable of God, and Revelation, the transcendence of which must be maintained. It is not surprising, therefore, that a problem of relations confronts us and that our solutions, while fundamentally the same, are sometimes formulated in different terms. For example, it is licit to take up a position on the plane of pure philosophy, in which case you can say that the problem indeed is not susceptible of an intelligible answer, and even that it never arises. The fact that a religious revelation has intervened between the Greeks and us cannot have altered the essence of philosophy. Those of our contemporaries for whom Scripture is a dead letter can continue to philosophize as they would have done, had they lived in the time of Plato and Aristotle. Even the Christian who philosophizes, in so far as he philosophizes, cannot adopt any other attitude. Unless he cuts himself off not only from the company of philosophers, but from philosophy itself, he can never borrow his principles elsewhere than from common reason, his philosophy can only be natural, there is for him no Christian philosophy. That, it seems to me, explains the opposition set up by so many Catholic philosophers against the notion of Christian philosophy, and not only explains it but, on this plane, justifies it.

But only on this plane does it justify it. For there are other planes, and first of all that of the history of philosophy. I only want to mention it here, by recalling that if the philosopher has to admit that the essence of philosophy is immutable, philosophers themselves are not. It is apparently a fact that the development of certain metaphysical theses attests the influence exercised by the Judeo-Christian Revelation on the orientation of western thought.[2] If the fact is real, history must take account of it; and what could be more legitimate for us than to use a particular name to designate the particular fact which it is establishing? Since it is a question of naming that definite state in which philosophy found itself from the fact that it had submitted to Christian influence, it would be hard to imagine a formula clearer than "Christian philosophy". Unless, therefore, historical proof be forthcoming that this influence never was exercised, one has no right to forbid the historian's using this formula to designate the effects it has produced.

No one has the right even to object that if a "Christian philosophy" is impossible in itself, it cannot be the object of history, for our concepts ought to be regulated by their objects; and if history shows that there were Christian philosophies, the notion therefore of Christian philosophy is indeed possible. It may be that it is inconceivable in itself from the point of view of philosophy, but philosophy is not the whole of thought. Theology also exists. After studying doctrines where reason judges everything unreservedly, the historian encounters others, and that from the 2nd century of our era, where it is formally affirmed that Revelation judges everything unreservedly, even what was considered throughout the ages as valid for, or capable of being defended by, the reason. In short, as soon as natural theology had come to be judged by a supernatural theology which at all times reserved the right to decide finally any problem that men could state on the subject of God and of their last ends, from that very moment a distinction was inevitable between the philosophies that revealed theology approved and those it condemned. Revealed wisdom discerns true wisdoms from false. Separating the philosophies that it accepts from those it rejects, guiding and regulating from above the efforts of human wisdoms to bear fruit, picking over and criticizing afterwards the results of the efforts, the science of Revelation, or theology, therefore, necessarily imposes a Christian point of view on philosophy. In short, if there is no Christian philosophy for the pagan philosopher, there is one for the Catholic theologian, and that explains why there may be one for history. The historian of philosophy can indeed, at his own risk, act as though this eighteen-centuries episode, which moreover still endures, were of no interest, but neither he nor the metaphysician can prevent its existing.

It is therefore with good reason that anyone speaking of Christian philosophy is charged with speaking as a theologian.[3] But if it is an historian that is being addressed, how can he be reproached for doing so, when he is forced to describe precisely an historical state of philosophy, wherein it finds its place explicitly in relation to a theology? And if it is a Catholic speaking to a Catholic, how would he justify that stupendous objection that "the expression *Christian philosophy* has no formally exact meaning"?[4] For whom has it no meaning? It may be that it has no meaning for the philosopher as such, but there exist analogous expressions which have meaning, and a very precise meaning, for the theologian. Catholic theology, and quite particularly that of St. Thomas, maintains very firmly that natures always remain formally what they are, but it distinguishes, beyond the diverse modalities of their existence, the different states in which they are found. If no point of view is accepted save that of the exact formal sense, what meaning will one find in the classical expression *natura corrupta?* A nature cannot be corrupted without ceasing to be a nature. Nor would it clear up anything to add that it is not *totaliter corrupta,* for an essence is indivisible, and the very idea of suppressing a part, while preserving the rest, has no sense.

The problem is completely changed, if we state it, as did St. Thomas, according to the diverse states in which nature can be found. In that case, by "the state of corrupt nature" will be meant that of a soul "which can no longer accomplish by its natural powers all the good of which its nature is capable".[5] Briefly, a corrupt nature is a sick nature; as a sick man remains a man; a sick reason a reason; a sick philosophy a philosophy. What then shall we say of a healed nature, a healed man, of a healed reason and philosophy? We simply have to remember, with St. Thomas, that the definition of a concept is a simple act, in which diverse terms participate in the simple unity of the very intellect which posits them. If any difficulty remains in expressions of this kind, it is certainly not that they forget nature, but rather that they grant too much to it, for it is not even true that our nature and our reason are absolutely healed. Subjected permanently to the *opus recreationis,* man is ordinarily described by St. Thomas only as being *sub gratia,* after having been under the Law. That, therefore, is a fact the consequences of which philosophy itself cannot escape: if it has been able to exist before the Law, and under the Law, it ought to exist today under grace, while waiting to be caught up in glory.[6] To be sure, there are and will, perhaps, always be philosophers without faith or law, but what they lack cannot confer any formal exactitude on what they possess. Philosophy is not more a philosophy when it is pagan than when it is Christian; it is then only an obscured philosophy. Philosophy is not less a philosophy when it is Christian than when it is pagan, nor is it more so; but it is better.

It is important not to overlook the consequences in which one would be inevitably implicated were he to refuse to admit such a thesis. To desire philosophy to cut itself off from every positive attachment to theology is to do one's best to put it in exactly the state in which certain Calvinists would like to keep it. It is conceivable that K. Barth would like it to be exclusively "mundane" in order to be faithful to its essence; the religious corruption of nature is for him an irremediable evil. It is harder to conceive a Catholic philosopher manifesting the same exaction. It would seem that *philosophy* becomes equivocal if the adjective *Christian* is added to it,[7] but philosophy has never been anything for philosophers but the search for wisdom; the word *wisdom* itself is therefore going to become equivocal, if the epithet *Christian* is added. Why wouldn't the expression "Christian wisdom" be just as lame, just as confused, as that of "Christian philosophy"? It exists, however; and if philosophy cannot pretend to it, it is because theology reserves the use of it to itself. Ethics is a part of philosophy; are we going to condemn as confused and lame the expression "Christian ethics"? The term *philosophy* has no more right to repel any adjective than the terms *wisdom* and *ethics;* and if it is thought that a rational research cannot remain rational while consenting to become Christian, it will practically be admitted that a nature cannot remain a nature if it is in a state of grace, nor a man remain a man if he agrees to become Christian.

It seems at least difficult to deny that there is really a problem here, and I am astonished that those who pass over it in silence believe, nevertheless, that the question can be easily settled.   Such an attitude might be comprehensible were it only a question of "pretending not to be a Catholic" for reasons of personal convenience or general opportunity. A tactic that, whatever be its value, always remains but a tactic; but we are here confronted with something quite different, since it is logical and abstract impossibilities that are being opposed to us.   It is necessary before anything else to remind those who raise them that human reason has for its proper function to think things as they are, and that it is unreasonable to hold that they cannot be as they are.   Everything that is real is possible; what is not so on one plane must be so on another, and it is up to us to find it there. No Catholic can define this plane without referring to the teaching of the Church.   What is disconcerting in such a controversy is that advantage may be taken of those very teachings to establish the right to do without them.

"What has faith to do with philosophy?" certain Catholics are heard to ask.   "What does it bring to it?   On certain questions philosophy is silent.   Then it is necessary to replace it by theology." [8]   What?   Does Catholic theology only really begin to speak when philosophy becomes silent? Thus, simply a "metaphilosophy" or "metametaphysics", it patiently and respectfully waits for natural reason to say its last word on God, before venturing to take up the discussion in its turn?   But we all know the Catholic position supposes the exact opposite.   Revelation speaks of *everything* which

philosophy speaks of, provided only that, by any title whatsoever, the glory of God and the salvation of men are involved; there is *nothing* that philosophy can say about God
and our last end that theology does not begin by deciding,
as to its essential truth, without paying the least attention as
to whether it suits our philosophy to take such a position.[9]
Yes, when philosophy is silent, theology still speaks, but
theology begins to speak even before philosophy consents to
be silent; and more important still, not only does it dare
to speak of the same thing of which philosophy speaks, but
after speaking of it in its own way, which is that of the divine
Word, it has the audacity to teach philosophy itself how a
philosophy worthy of the name ought to speak of it.

Therein, I think, lies the rock of scandal. Yet I confess, I am at a loss to understand why, if the one scandalized
is a Catholic. All our theologians teach that theology has
the right to use philosophy, in view of the ends proper to it;
they all do it, to such an extent that the clearest expositions
of their most original philosophical theses are often found
in their theological works. What explanation can be given
for so constant a phenomenon except that a theologian is
practically obliged to intervene directly in philosophical disputes, and to settle them as a philosopher, if he wants to get
for himself the materials necessary for his work as a theologian? It is therefore a fact that Catholic theology is vitally
concerned in watching over the work of the philosopher and,
if he does it badly, repairing it for him. Such is, moreover,
the explanation of the self-imposed effort of St. Albert the
Great in drawing up his monumental philosophical encyclo-
pedia, of St. Thomas Aquinas in writing his commentaries
on Aristotle, and Duns Scotus his *Metaphysical Questions*.
Certainly, they did these things as philosophers, but never-

theless for theology. The devil, in clerical garb, who came one day to reproach Saint Albert for busying himself with these things—and he a Christian, priest and monk—could pretend to be deceived by them: he even would have been deceived in all sincerity if he were really a monk making himself the devil's advocate, and there have always been some of them to do so. It is not advisable to bring grist to their mills. By permitting it to be thought that our great theologians of the Middle Ages attacked the study of the sciences and of philosophy just as though they were not theologians, you are practically granting those to be right who see in Albert the Great "a physician preoccupied with giving himself a world system, an explanation of phenomena, apart from religion, and independent of it", while all that Saint Thomas would have done was to formulate in a precise theory "the separatism already admitted and practiced by Albert the Great".[10]   That is nothing less than to accuse two theologians, two saints, two doctors of the Church, with having betrayed their theological office. We cannot prevent the making of such accusations, but we ought to do our best not to provoke them; and they will be provoked every time the thought of these men is dechristianized, by presenting it just as pagan as its adversaries could wish it to be, that they might have the right to reject it.

I am not unaware of the resources still left for the adversaries of Christian philosophy to condemn its very notion. Let it be, they will say: let us admit that these theologians have engaged in philosophy in view of their theology. Since it was in philosophy, they were, therefore, really only philosophers, while so engaged. Everything evidently depends here on the conditions necessary for rational activity to be qualified as philosophical. In the 18th century, a Philosopher was essentially a man who thought *against* all revealed religion; today the minimum required of a philosopher is that he think *outside* all revealed religion. I willingly recognize that to be a fact, having experienced it for too many years to be oblivious to it; but I confess I do not see why it ought to be accepted by Catholic thinkers as an inevitable exigency. The only surprising thing about the matter is that some of them think they are obliged to do so. When it is suggested by some theologians that from the moment that a philosophy is "guided" by faith, it becomes a theology;[11] or when it is declared: "If my reason is too weak to solve all the problems which philosophy states, I need faith; but I do not understand how a research remains purely rational while being directed, orientated by faith",[12] such declarations are extremely embarrassing to simple laymen. Their normal rôle ought to be to defend philosophy against the encroachments of theology, not theology against what seems to be an excessive modesty on the part of theologians. The thing has to be done, however, even at the risk of incurring some ridicule, for the interests at stake are such that I know of none greater.

Let us point out, therefore, to those who express themselves as if they had forgotten it, that the attitude which they recommend can with difficulty be made to agree with that prescribed by the Church, whose members they are. The encyclical *Aeterni Patris* is in reality the text with which they are at variance: not what one or another among us can say on these matters, but this document, which defines so forcefully the position of Catholicism in these matters. After recalling that philosophy, when properly used, can prepare those, who study it, for receiving faith, Leo XIII explains why it may render such a service. The reason, he says, is that, in whatever relates to things divine, God has not only revealed by the light of faith those truths which the human intelligence is incapable of attaining, "but He has manifested some, which are not beyond the power of reason to grasp, in order that, the authority of God being joined to them, they might be known by all immediately and without error". Up to this point, I suppose, we are all ready to agree. But let us be careful about what follows. The Encyclical does not advise merely gathering from the works of pagan authors whatever testifies to the truth of these revealed teachings, as all the Christian doctors have done. It explicitly adds this: "that if natural reason has produced such an abundant harvest before being fertilized by the virtue of Christ, it will certainly bring forth a much richer one, now that the grace of the Saviour has restored and augmented the natural faculties of human thought. Who therefore would not see that, by a philosophy of this kind, a simple and easy path is opened towards faith?" And so in my turn, I ask: On which of these points are we not agreed? It is here indeed a question of philosophy: *philosophia;* of a philosophy which is truly the work of natural reason: *naturalis ratio;* of a natural philosophy, however, which facilitates the access to faith; *iter ad fidem aperire;* which can do so today better than ever because the grace of Christ has restored and augmented the powers of natural reason: *instauravit et auxit.* Such is the exercise of reason that the title of the Encyclical designates by the name of *Christian philosophy;* therefore it is simply a question of knowing whether to admit or deny that the exercise of natural reason assisted by Revelation is still a natural exercise of it, and whether the philosophy it begets still deserves the name philosophy?

Once this point is settled, another remains. Does the

action exercised by the grace of Christ on the philosopher's reason include Revelation or not? To this very problem the Encyclical gives an equally clear answer, and one which in no way authorizes the characteristics of a purely "negative" standard that some would like to attribute to Revelation.[13] Let one read again the following words: "Those who join submission to the Christian faith to the study of philosophy, are those who philosophise in the best possible manner, since the splendor of the divine truths, accepted by the soul, assists the intelligence itself, from which it not only does not detract anything, but actually adds considerably to its nobility, penetration and stability." How, may I ask, can the rays of divine truth increase the stability and penetration of the natural intellect, without making it see the truth towards which it ought to bend its course, and consequently directing it there?

That is the basis of the dispute and what gives it its real significance. I am reproached with "being rabid" in maintaining the expression Christian philosophy; will I be excused for asking why some other are "furious" in eliminating it? My personal reasons are no secret: they rest on a story, which is brief, and so simple that I am going to tell it without hoping that it will be believed. I had written the first volume of the *Spirit of Mediaeval Philosophy*,[14] from what has become in it Chapter III to the end, without thinking of the notion of Christian philosophy. It was then that the idea struck me; and as it seemed to me to give a unity to the philosophy which I was in the act of describing, I wrote the first two chapters on that notion. I was quite satisfied with my discovery when, studying afterwards the documents relative to this notion and coming across the Encyclical *Aeterni Patris*, which I had completely forgotten, I perceived that the very idea that I was trying to justify in two volumes, twenty lectures, and I don't know how many notes, was exactly what the Encyclical would have sufficed to teach me, implying as it does the very interpretation of mediaeval philosophy that I was proposing.

I admit the incident left me crestfallen. I realized instantly that anyone at all could henceforth prove, according to the infallible rules of the "Critical Method", that my two volumes were simply apologetical books, without proper scientific value, a sort of pseudo-historical commentary of the Encyclical *Aeterni Patris*. I would do so myself, did I find it necessary; if others do it, I can make no answer except that that was not the way things happened. That I would not easily forget the incident, is only what might be expected. This notion of Christian philosophy, which had cost me so much trouble to justify from the facts, and which was brought back to my memory by my colleague M. E. Bréhier's denying its existence, had, however, been imposed on me at the end of a long research, from which a little attention to the teaching of the Church could have dispensed me. I do not think I have been overzealous in maintaining it; on the contrary, more than thirty studies devoted to this discussion, and in some cases even books, have remained without so much as a word in reply on my part; but not replying was a mistake, and it is rather for that that I should be blamed. I am held to answer not only because of what I think is the historical truth, but because of what I believe is the Catholic truth. After all, the title of Encyclical is there; I didn't invent it, and, supposing that I am obstinate in speaking of *philosophia christiana,* the least that I can say to the Catholic philosophers who reproach me for it is that their attitude is rather suprising. For Leo XIII is not content merely with writing the Encyclical, he has prescribed that Catholic schools be conformed to it.[15] I repeat, therefore, simply for being convinced of it by history, that the faith has truly shone on the waves of error "as a friendly star, which, without fear of error, points out the port of truth". If you tell me that this *sidus amicum* of which the Encyclical speaks is a star which does not orientate or that it shows the port of truth to reason without guiding it there, I must simply confess I no longer know the meaning of the simplest words. A lay person is excusable for getting lost in these matters; but since the philosophers who criticize me are at the same time Catholic theologians, they will surely take the trouble of explaining it to me.

Now in order for the explanations to be of any use, it is to be hoped that we both talk about the same things. There is no question of establishing some kind of a hybrid, a "sort of speculation intermediary between philosophy as such and theology".[16] Arguments of this kind are irrefutable, since what they deny does not exist. Who has ever dreamed of inventing this monster? Quite to the contrary, those who speak of "Christian philosophy" and the Encyclical *Aeterni Patris* in the first place, maintain at the same time as an unshakable principle that philosophy and theology are two sciences formally distinct both by their principles and by their objects. There is, therefore, nothing, nor is it proposed to introduce anything, between the one and the other. What we say about God is philosophy or theology, according as it is based on reason or on faith. Formally, therefore, a philosophy can be only philosophy, and never theology, but it does not follow that it cannot be Christian and, if it is only agreed, bear that name.

For such, in the last analysis, is the state in which it

exists, and which those who refuse to call it Christian do not describe very exactly.   They picture for us a philosophy doing just fine in its own line, with theology discreetly suggesting the odd idea, notion and possibility, for which reason is indeed obliged.[17]   Truth to tell, in all this, philosophy makes use of theology, rather than the reverse.   For all I know a philosopher may have to talk like that in order to feel he is a philosopher, but it certainly is not the way a theologian would speak.   There is no hesitation on his part as to whether the philosophy of the Christian is or is not in a state defined by the very essence of Christianity, nor as to what that state is.   Let us call things by their names; it is, as we say, "in service".   The expression may seem disagreeable, but it denotes exactly what it means, and the preceding discussion sufficiently shows that the time has come for restoring it. Let us say rather that it has returned, for its return is periodic.   We feel quite certain that St. Thomas never recoiled from the word: theology is a queen, the other sciences are called her handmaids (*aliae scientiae dicuntur ancillae ejus*), and philosophy is no exception.   For the theologian it also is a servant, and Pope Gregory IX, who was by no means an obscurantist, was even harder in his expressions.   Those "*theophantes*" whom he reproached for according too many rights to philosophy, instead of "reducing all understanding into captivity in the service of Christ", according to the words of St. Paul,[18] subject the head to the tail "and oblige the queen to serve the servant".   Pius IX and Pius X have purposely taken up the same expression and recalled that, in regard to everything that pertains to religion, the rôle of philosophy "is not to dominate but to serve".   Unless, therefore, the existence of God, His Unity, Creative Power, and all the attributes knowable by natural reason, but revealed by God Himself, which are prescribed to all as things that must be believed, are excluded from those things *quae ad religionem pertinent*, it seems hardly possible to avoid the conclusion that the natural theology of the Christian is at the service of his supernatural theology. But it is precisely in this state of service that it finds itself as philosophy. That at least is what the history of its rebirth in the middle ages teaches us and what could still be the cause of its rebirth among us. If Albert the Great and St. Thomas may be called the authors of that rebirth, it is because they worked energetically to distinguish the philosophical from the theological, and to restore to honour a speculation worthy of the name of philosophy. It is, however, above all for the sake of theology that they rendered this great service to philosophy. In order that philosophy might serve, it was necessary first of all that it exist as philosophy, and so they began by freeing it patiently from its theological gangue, giving it its charter, which recognized rights but also prescribed duties. We have the tendency today to retain nothing but the rights, yet the duties still remain and it is for theology to remind us of them.

The theology of St. Thomas Aquinas did so with a precision forestalling any pretension of not knowing it on the part of anyone who professes his doctrine. To be sure, faith for him presupposes natural knowledge as grace presupposes nature, but, precisely, faith acts with regard to reason as grace with regard to nature; it subjects it to itself. And let us note well that it is precisely the order of natural knowledge that is here in question: the natural knowledge, which faith presupposes and reason can prove, is upheld by faith *(fidei substernitur naturalis cognitio quam fides praesupponit et ratio probare potest)*. Thus natural reason is subjected to faith, even when it is a question of knowing that God exists: *Deum esse,* that He is One, Intelligent, Incorporeal, etc. Why? Among other reasons, because man, quite naturally ordered though he be to the divine, cannot raise himself to it by himself. He needs a professor, a pedagogue; and since everybody hasn't one at his disposal, God has provided for that by offering to all the light of faith which raises their thought to truths of this order.[19] There is the real doctrine of St. Thomas, concerning which he never wavered. In matters of natural theology faith is not only possible, it is even absolutely *sufficiens,* for all men could be saved without philosophy. The natural light, on the contrary, is not *sufficiens,* because it is fallible, darkened, and because it needs God Himself in order to recover itself. It is not, then, simply a question of an abstract classification, but indeed of a real subordination.

Perhaps it is nothing but a question of our resuming a salutary habit: that of speaking as Christians in our Christian affairs. That is indeed what Pope Leo XIII means to recall to us when he invites us to restore to honour the rights of Christian philosophy. The complaint is voiced that this philosophy exists only for Christians. That is possible all right, but how would that prove that it does not exist at all? As the future Cardinal Ehrle justly pointed out, in a series of articles on *The Papal Encyclical of the 4th of August 1879 and the restoration of Christian philosophy,* "by its title and contents, the Encyclical properly interests only the realms within the jurisdiction of the Church, speaks directly only to believing members of the great Christian family".[20] Pope Leo XIII was not therefore particularly preoccupied in defining the formal essence of philosophy and theology—although he did not neglect to do that in its proper place—but in giving to the faithful, of whom he is the father, the counsels which he deemed necessary regarding the restoration of a Christian state of philosophy. He would, without doubt, have been surprised, had he been given to understand that a day would come when those whom he had charged with the restoration of Christian philosophy would teach, on the authority of his name, that the expression Christian philosophy "had no meaning". Ehrle, on the contrary, immediately grasped the sense and the import of this important document, when he underlined the words, "with Christian Revelation was given first a new standard, infallible and supreme for all human science; secondly, the impulse towards the construction of a new and Christian philosophy. The system of philosophy, which is above everything else Christian in principle, and the beginnings of which consequently stretch back into the past to the very birth of Christianity, can alone today pretend to the truth and to an exclusive validity".[21] It would be difficult to penetrate more profoundly into the intimate spirit of a text than has been here done by one whom we all recognize as one of the masters of the history of mediaeval thought. He would not try to minimize the subjection of philosophy to theology with the pretense of thereby better defending it: "The fact that the science of faith (or theology) has need of the help of philosophy does not change their relation of dependence any more than the fact that a mistress has need of her servant suffices to change the servant into the mistress. Other things being equal, the philosophy most radically submissive to this direction, possesses also the greatest guarantee of truth. On the contrary, every system of philosophical doctrine of which this submission is not a fundamental principle, must be presumed to have sinned from the very start". That is, then, not merely a question, as some would like to have us believe, of getting a factual agreement, be it ever so complete, between the teachings of reason and those of faith: "From what has gone before, we are fully justified in speaking of the relation of philosophy to theology as one of *service*. To be sure, this expression easily lends itself to a false interpretation. There is, however, in this dependence nothing dishonouring, nothing humiliating for science; it is not a case here of a heavy yoke, of shackles which restrain real and veritable liberty. No, there is but a direction and an assistance eminently beneficent and desirable. Consequently the more confidently philosophical research entrusts itself to this direction, the more zealously it draws profit from this assistance, the greater and firmer also will be its progress".[22] That is what the Encyclical *Aeterni Patris* means and consequently also as far as it is necessary to go.

It is perhaps there that the ultimate justification of its title is to be found. That one may get along without a name to designate a philosophy disposed to receive complacently the discreet suggestions of a faith is, strictly speaking, conceivable, but he who thinks that "every system of philosophy in order to be able to be true, must be Christian in principle",[23] will naturally experience the need, in order to express the fundamental character of this moral necessity, of finding a name for the philosophy which submits to it. Not that he pretends to invent a new genus of knowledge of God, which would be neither faith nor reason, but the species philosophy can comprehend different families; and if there is a family which is distinguished from the others in that it alone takes advantage of every means of being true, the internal relation uniting it to the guarantee of which it makes use has the right to figure in the name which designates it.

It is not only legitimate, it is necessary. We are dealing, therefore, with a notion logically possible and susceptible of definition. Christian philosophy is a philosophy which, though formally distinguishing the two orders, considers Christian Revelation to be an indispensable guide to truth.[24]

It is rather disturbing for us that, instead of hearing these fundamental truths taught to us as first certitudes, we have today to fight for them, sometimes even against those from whom it seems that we ought to be getting them. It is, alas, because we feel ourselves each day so threatened in the goods without which man cannot live that we have to seek the explanation for our misery, that we may know whence will come salvation. It were hard to be mistaken about that cause, for our misery is nothing but that of fallen man. The danger which is perpetually ours is the same to which succumb "those partisans, or rather those adorers of human reason, who propose it to themselves as a sure mistress and, under its guidance, promise themselves all success, forgetting without doubt how serious and cruel is the wound inflicted on human nature by the fall of our first parent: those shadows which are shed on our thought, and this will which henceforth inclines towards evil. Whence it happened that the most celebrated philosophers of antiquity, although they wrote many fine things, nevertheless spoiled their doctrines, by most serious errors. Whence also that incessant combat that we experience within ourselves, and of which the apostle speaks: *Sentio in membris meis legem repugnantem legi mentis meae.*" Thus does Pius IX[25] express himself in words of admirable plenitude, and the Christian hearing them, seeing his evil described with that infallible authority, begins to hope for the remedy for it.

Here it is: "The progress of the sciences and the success

in avoiding or refuting the miserable errors of our era, entirely depends on our intimate adherence to the revealed
truths, which the Church teaches . . . It is by leaning on this
truth that true and wise Catholics have been able safely to
cultivate the sciences, expound them, render them useful and
certain. This can be secured only if human reason, even
within its own limits and pursuing the study of those truths
which it can attain by its own powers and faculties, reveres
profoundly, as is fitting, the infallible and uncreated light
of the divine intellect, which shines in a marvellous way in
all directions in Christian Revelation. Although indeed
those natural disciplines are established on their own principles, such as reason knows them, yet it is necessary that the
Catholics who cultivate them keep before their eyes Divine
Revelation as a guiding star".[26] *Veluti stella retrix*, said
Pius IX: *velut sidus amicum*, Leo XIII was to repeat. Between their authorized word and that of men who deny that
Revelation orientates or directs them, no hesitation is possible. For not only is it first of all a question for us of
being Catholics and, since such is the attitude which the
Church prescribes for us, we must conform ourselves to it,
even if it cost us philosophy; but as a matter of fact, quite to
the contrary, we will certainly lose philosophy unless we conform ourselves to it. It will be difficult to make us believe
that what makes a philosophy to be true prevents it from
being a true philosophy. It is by being paganized that
nature is lost, as it is by being christianized that it is saved,
and it remains for us to consider the duties this principle
imposes on us.

V

THE INTELLIGENCE IN THE SERV-
ICE OF CHRIST THE KING

"LOVE not the world, nor the things which are in the world. If any man love the world, the charity of the Father is not in him. For all that is in the world is the concupiscence of the flesh, and the concupiscence of the eyes, and the pride of life; which is not of the Father, but is of the world. And the world passeth away, and the concupiscence thereof: but he that doth the will of God abideth forever." Bossuet recalls these words of the first Epistle of John[1] at the end of his *Treatise on Concupiscence*, and he adds to them this brief but pithy commentary: "the last words of this Apostle show us that the world, of which he is here speaking, is those who prefer visible and transient things to those invisible and everlasting". Allow me to add simply in my turn, that if we attain to an understanding of the meaning of this definition, the mighty problem we have to examine together will resolve itself.

We are in the world; whether we like it or not, it is a fact, and to be there or not to be there does not depend on us; but we ought not to be of the world. How is it possible to be in the world without being of it? That is the problem which has haunted the Christian conscience since the foundation of the Church, and which looms particularly large with regard to our intelligence. For it is quite true that the

Christian life offers us a radical solution of this difficulty: to leave the world, to renounce it completely by taking refuge in the monastic life. But in the first place, states of perfection will always remain the portion of an élite; but more important still, the perfect themselves flee from the world in order to save it by saving themselves, and it is a remarkable fact that the world doesn't always even permit them to save it. There will always be among us souls desirous of fleeing from the world, but it is by no means certain that the world will always permit them to flee from it; for not only does the world affirm itself, it does not even want to admit that some renounce it. That is the cruelest injury that can be inflicted on it. Now, the Christian use of the intelligence is an injury of the same sort, and perhaps, among all, that which wounds it most profoundly; for the more it takes account of the fact that the intelligence is the highest thing in man, the more it longs to arrogate its homage and subject it to itself alone. To deny it this homage is the first intellectual duty of the Christian. Why and how? That is what we have to find out.

The everlasting protest of the world against Christians is that they scorn it, and that by scorning it they misunderstand what constitutes the proper value of its nature: its goodness, its beauty and its intelligibility. That explains the ceaseless reproaches directed against us, in the name of philosophy, of history and of science: Christianity refuses to take the whole man, and, under the pretext of making him better, it mutilates him, forcing him to close his eyes to things that constitute the excellence of nature and life, to misunderstand the progress of society throughout history and to hold suspect science which progressively discloses the laws of nature and those of societies. These reproaches, repeatedly flung at us, are so familiar as to cease to interest us; nevertheless it is our duty never to cease replying to them, and above all never to lose sight ourselves of what is the reply to them. Yes, Christianity is a radical condemnation of the world, but it is at the same time an unreserved approbation of nature; for the world is not nature, it is nature shaping its course without God.

What is true of nature is eminently true of the intelligence, the crown of nature. In the evening of creation, God looked at His work and He judged, says the Scripture, that all that was very good. But what was best in His work was man, created to His image and likeness; and if we seek the basis of this divine likeness, we find it, says Saint Augustine, *in mente*: in thought. Let us go further, still following the same doctor: we find that this likeness is in that part of thought which is, so to speak, the summit, that by which, in contact with the divine light of which it is a sort of reflection, it conceives truth. To seize truth here below by the intelligence, be it in an obscure and partial manner, while waiting to see it in its complete splendour—such is man's destiny according to Christianity. Indeed far from scorning knowledge, it cherishes it: *intellectum valde ama*.

Unless, therefore, a person pretends to know better than Saint Augustine what Christianity is, he cannot reproach us with betraying it or accommodating it to the needs of the cause by following the advice of this saint: love intelligence, and love it very much. The truth is that if we love the intelligence as much as our adversaries, and sometimes even more, we do not love it in the same way. There is a love of the intelligence which consists in turning it towards visible and transient things: that belongs to the world; but there is another which consists in turning it towards the invisible and eternal: that belongs to Christians. It is, therefore, ours; and if we prefer it to the first, it is because it does not deny us anything the first would give us, and yet it overwhelms us with everything which the other is incapable of giving us.

That there is something in Christianity which its adversaries do not succeed in grasping is clearly seen in the contradictory character of the objections that they address to it, but it is also a consolation for us to note that their objections rest on such misunderstandings. For they reproach it with putting man at the center of everything, but also with underestimating his greatness; and I am willing to admit that we may be mistaken in saying one thing or the other, but not in saying them both at the same time. And what is true of man in general is true of the intelligence in particular. I could let a person reproach Saint Thomas Aquinas with having betrayed the spirit of Christianity by unduly exalting the rights of the intelligence, or reproach him for having betrayed the spirit of philosophy by unduly exalting the rights of faith, but I cannot understand how he could do both at the same time. What mystery, therefore, must be hidden in the depths of the Christian man, that his most spontaneous and unvaried steps seem so mysterious to those who observe them from without!

*   *   *

This mystery, for it is really a mystery, is the mystery of Jesus Christ. It is enough to be informed, no matter how vaguely, as to what Christianity is, in order to know in what this mystery consists. By the Incarnation, God became man, that is to say the two natures, divine and human, are found united in the person of Christ. What is less well known to those who adhere to this mystery by faith is the astonishing transformation which He introduced into all nature and consequently into the manner in which we must henceforth conceive it.   One ought rather to say the astonishing trans-formations, for this mystery includes in it so many others that one would never have done considering the consequences of it.

Let us be content here with examining one of them: that which leads us directly to the heart of our subject. From the moment human nature was assumed by the divine nature in the person of Christ, God no longer dominates and governs nature solely as God, but also as man.   If, among all men there is one who truly merits the title of Man-God, how could such a one not be also the chief and the sovereign of all the others, in short, their king?   That is why Christ is not only the spiritual sovereign of the world, but also its temporal sovereign.   But we know, on the other hand, that the Church is the mystical body of Christ: that its faithful are the members of this mystical body, that is to say, accord-ing to the doctrine of Saint Paul: the members of Christ; all the faithful are, therefore, in so far as they are members of Christ, priests and kings: *"Et quod est amplius,"* says Saint Thomas, *"omnes Christi fideles, in quantum sunt membra ejus, reges et sacerdotes dicuntur."* [2]   There is, then, hence-forth, in every Christian, as an image, and even as a partici-pation of this supreme mystery, humanity divinized by grace, reclothed, in its very misery, by a dignity at once sacerdo-tal and royal, which makes up the mystery of the Christian man.

Of this prodigious transformation of nature by the In-carnation we have an interpretation of incomparable pro-fundity in Pascal, for that is what gives to his work the plenitude of its meaning.   That we know God only through the person of Christ, Who was God Himself living, speaking, and acting among us, God showing Himself as man to men in order to be known by them, is too evident; but the great discovery, or rediscovery of Pascal, is to have understood that the Incarnation, by profoundly changing the nature of man, has become the only means that there is for us to understand man. Such a truth gives a new meaning to our nature, to our birth, to our end. "Not only", wrote Pascal, "do we only understand God through Jesus Christ, but we only understand ourselves through Jesus Christ. We understand life and death only through Jesus Christ. Outside of Jesus Christ we know not what life is, nor death, nor God, nor ourselves." [3]

Let us apply these principles to the exercise of our intelligence; we shall immediately see that that of the Christian, as opposed to one which knows not Jesus Christ, knows itself to be fallen and restored, incapable consequently of yielding its full return without grace, and, in this sense, just as the royalty of Christ dominates the order of nature and the order of society, so also it dominates the order of the intelligence. Perhaps we Catholics have forgotten it too much; perhaps we have never even truly understood it, and if ever there was a time that needed to understand it, it is indeed our own.

What, in fact, does this mystery teach us in regard to the ends and the nature of the intelligence?

Like the nature which it crowns, the intelligence is good; but it is only so if, by it and in it, the whole nature turns towards its end, which is to conform itself to God. But, by taking itself as its own end, the intelligence has turned away from God, turning nature with it, and grace alone can aid both of them in returning to what is really their end, since it is their origin. The "world" is just this refusal to participate in grace which separates nature from God, and the intelligence itself is of the world in so far as it joins with it in rejecting grace. The intelligence which accepts grace is that of the Christian. And it is in the abandonment of precisely this Christian state of the intelligence that the world, because of its hate for it, ever urges us to accompany it.

That is what constitutes the real danger for us. We have no doubts concerning the truth of Christianity; we are firmly resolved to think as Christians; but do we know what must be done in order to accomplish that? Do we even know exactly in what Christianity consists? The first Christians knew it, because Christianity then was very near its beginnings, and the adversary against which it fought could not be unknown or misconceived by anyone; it was paganism, that is to say, ignorance at once of sin which damns and the grace of Jesus Christ which saves. That is why the Church, not only then but throughout the ages, has especially recalled to men the corruption of nature by sin, the weakness of reason without Revelation, the impotence of the will to do good when it is not aided by grace. When Saint Augustine battled against Pelagius, who called himself Christian and thought himself Christian, it was against an attempt of paganism to restore the ancient naturalism and introduce it into the very heart of Christianity, that the great doctor fought. The naturalism of the Renaissance was another attempt of the same kind and we are still, today, in a world which believes itself naturally healthy, just and good, because, having forgotten sin and grace, it takes its corruption for the rule of nature itself.

There is nothing in all that which the Christian may

not and even ought not to expect. We know that the battle of good against evil will end only with the world itself. What is more serious is that paganism may ceaselessly try to penetrate within Christianity itself, as in the time of Pelagius, and may succeed in the attempt. That is a never-ending danger for us and one which we can avoid only with great difficulty. To live as Christians, to feel as Christians, to think as Christians in a society which is not Christian, when we see, hear and read almost nothing which does not offend or contradict Christianity; when especially life places an obligation on us, and charity often gives us the duty of not making a visible break with the ideas and customs that we reprove, all that is difficult and hardly possible. That is also the reason why we are continually tempted to diminish or adapt our truth, in order to lessen the distance which separates our ways of thinking from those of the world, or indeed, and sometimes in all sincerity, in the hope of rendering Christianity more acceptable to the world and of seconding its work of salvation.

Hence the errors, the looseness of thought and the compromises against which, at all times, the zeal of certain reformers has rebelled. The restoration of Christianity to the purity of its essence was in fact the first intention of Luther and Calvin; such is still today that of the illustrious Calvinistic theologian, Karl Barth, who employs all his powers to purify liberal Protestantism from naturalism, and to restore the Reform itself to the unconditional respect of the word of God. We all know how energetically he pursues that aim. God speaks, says K. Barth; man listens and repeats what God has said. Unfortunately, as is inevitable from the moment that a man sets himself up as His interpreter: God speaks, the Barthian listens and repeats what

Barth has said. That is why, if we believe this new gospel of his, God would be reputed as having said that, ever since the first sin, nature is so totally corrupted that nothing of it remains but its very corruption, a mass of perdition which grace can indeed still pardon, but which nothing henceforth could ever heal. Thus, then, in order the better to fight against paganism and Pelagianism, this doctrine invites us to despair of nature, to renounce all effort to save reason and rechristianize it.

It is these two perils which ceaselessly plague us, and which, lest our thought be free from all attack, sometimes reduce us to a state of uncertainty as to what is or is not Christian. We forget the golden rule which decides all issues and dissipates every confusion, and one which we ought to have ever present to thought as the light which no obscurity can resist. It is that Catholicism teaches before everything the restoration of wounded nature by the grace of Jesus Christ. The restoration of nature: so there must be a nature, and of what value, since it is the work of a God, Who created it and re-created it by repurchasing it at the price of His own Blood! Thus grace presupposes nature, and the excellence of nature which it comes to heal and transfigure. As opposed to Calvinism and Lutheranism, the Church refuses to despair of nature, as if sin had totally corrupted it, but She tenderly bends over it, to heal its sores and save it. The God of our Church is not only a judge Who pardons, He is a judge Who can pardon only because He is first a doctor Who heals. But if She doesn't despair of nature, neither does the Church hope that it can heal itself. Just as She opposes the despair of Calvinism, so too She opposes the foolish hope of naturalism, which seeks in the malady itself the principle of its cure. The truth of

Catholicism is not a mean between two errors, which would
participate in both the one and the other, but a real truth,
that is to say a peak, from which it is possible to discover
both what the errors are and what makes them to be so.
For the Calvinist, a Catholic is so respectful of nature that
he is in nothing distinguished from a pagan, save by an ad-
ditional blindness which makes him degrade even Christianity itself into paganism. But the Catholic well knows that
there is nothing in that, and that it is the Calvinist who, con-
founding nature with the world, can no longer love nature
under the world which clothes it, that is to say, love the work
of God while hating sin which deforms it. For the pagan,
the Christian saint is an enemy of nature, who rushes furi-
ously in a foolish rage to torture it and even to mutilate it;
but the Catholic knows well that he chastises nature only
out of love for it: the evil which he fights against has entered
too deeply into it to be able to be plucked out of it without
making it suffer. Just as Calvinism despairs of nature while
believing to despair only of its corruption, so naturalism puts
its hope only in corruption when it thinks it is putting it in
nature. Catholicism alone knows exactly what is nature, and
what is the world, and what is grace, but it knows it only
because it keeps its eyes fixed on the concrete union of nature
and of grace in the Redeemer of nature, the person of Jesus
Christ.

To imitate the Church ought to be our rule, if we wish
to put our intelligence at the service of Christ the King.
For, to serve Him, is to unite our efforts to His; to make
ourselves, according to the word of Saint Paul, His coop-
erators, that is to say, work with Him, or permit Him to
work in us and through us for the salvation of the intelligence blinded by sin. But to work thus, it will be necessary

for us to follow the example He Himself gives us: to free the nature which the world hides from us, to make that use of the intelligence to which God destined it when creating it.

It is here, it seems to me, that we have to make a return on ourselves, to ask ourselves if we are doing our duty and especially if we are doing it well. We have all met, either in history or indeed round about us, Christians who believe they are rendering homage to God by affecting, in regard to science, philosophy and art, an indifference which sometimes approaches contempt. But this contempt may express either supreme greatness or supreme littleness. I like to be told that all philosophy is not worth an hour of trouble, when he who tells me so is called Pascal, that is to say, a man who is at once one of the greatest philosophers, one of the greatest scientists, and one of the greatest artists of all time. A person always has the right to disdain what he surpasses, especially if what he disdains is not so much the thing loved as the excessive attachment which enslaves us to it. Pascal despised neither science nor philosophy, but he never pardoned them for having once hidden from him the most profound mystery of charity. Let us be careful, therefore, we who are not Pascal, of despising what perhaps surpasses us, for science is one of the highest praises of God: the understanding of what God has made.

That is not all. No matter how high science may be, it is only too clear that Jesus Christ did not come to save men by science or philosophy; He came to save all men, *even* philosophers and scientists; and though these human activities are not indispensable to salvation, yet even they have need of being saved as does this whole order of nature which grace has come to repurchase. But it is necessary to be careful not to save them by an indiscreet zeal, which, under the pretense of purifying them more completely, would only result in corrupting their essences. There is reason to fear that this fault is committed quite often, and that with the best intentions in the world, in view of what certain defenders of the faith call the apologetical use of science. An excellent formula, no doubt, yet only when one knows not only what science is, but also what apologetics is.

To be an efficacious apologist, it is necessary first to be a theologian; I will even say, an excellent theologian. That is rarer than we might think, which will be a scandal to those who speak of theology only by hearsay, or are content with reciting its formulae without having taken time to plumb their significance. But if one wishes to make an apologetic from science, it is not even sufficient that he be an excellent theologian; he must also be an excellent savant. I say savant advisedly, and not merely an intelligent and cultivated man more or less anointed by science. If one wishes to practice science for God, the first condition is to practice science for itself, or as if one practiced it for itself, since that is the only way of acquiring it. The same holds for philosophy. It is self-delusion to think to serve God by taking a certain number of formulae which bespeak what one knows ought to be said, without understanding why what they say is true. It is not even serving Him to denounce errors, however false they may be, while showing that one does not even understand in what they are false. At least we can say that it is not serving Him as a savant or as a philosopher, which is all we are for the moment concerned in showing. And I will add that the same thing holds for art, for it is necessary to possess it before pretending to put it at the service of God. We are told that it is faith which constructed the cathedrals of the middle ages. Without doubt, but faith would have constructed nothing at all if there had not also been architects; and if it is true that the façade of Notre Dame of Paris is a yearning of the soul towards God, that does not prevent its being also a geometrical work. It is necessary to know geometry in order to construct a façade which may be an act of love.

Catholics, who confess the eminent value of nature because it is a work of God, let us therefore show our respect for it by positing as the first rule of our action, that *piety never dispenses with technique*. For technique is that without which even the most lively piety is incapable of using nature for God. No one, nor anything, obliges the Christian to busy himself with science, art or philosophy, for other ways of serving God are not wanting; but *if that is the way of serving God that he has chosen*, the end itself, which he proposes for himself in studying them, binds him to excellence. He is bound by the very intention which guides him, to become a good savant, a good philosopher or a good artist. That is for him the only way of becoming a good servant.

Such is, after all, the teaching of the Church and the example She has transmitted to us. Did not Saint Paul say that "the invisible perfections of God, His eternal power and dignity are, since the creation of the world, rendered visible to the intelligence by means of His works"? That is why so many doctors, who were at the same time savants, lovingly bent over the work of creation. For them, to study it is to study God in His works; never did a Saint Albert the Great think to know enough about nature, because the better he knew it, the better also he knew God. But there are not two ways of knowing it: a person possesses science or he doesn't possess it, he studies things scientifically or is resigned to never knowing anything about them. Saint Albert the Great became, therefore, first of all a savant, in the proper sense of the term. Of those who are astonished or scandalized, he says that, brute beasts, they blaspheme what they do not know. He knows what he is doing: he does not wait until the care of repairing an evil already committed obliges him to busy himself in his turn with science in order to remedy it. He does not believe in the policy of letting the adversaries do everything with the intention of later joining their school in order to learn laboriously the use of the weapons that will be turned against them. Albert studied the sciences against no one, but for God. When you find a man of that sort, he does not waste his time proving that the teaching of science does not contradict that of the Church: he suppresses the question by his example, showing the world that a man can be a man of science, because he is a man of God. Such is also the attitude the Church recommends to us. By making Saint Albert the Great the patron of Catholic schools, She reminds us permanently that these schools ought never be afraid of placing the level of their teaching and of their scientific exigencies too high. Everything is worth the trouble of being well done, that is worth the trouble of being done for God.

Still we must never forget that it is for Him that it is being done, and to forget that is the second danger which threatens us. To serve God by science or art, it is necessary to begin by practicing them *as if* these disciplines were in themselves their own ends; and it is difficult to make such an effort without being taken in. So much the more difficult is it when we are surrounded by savants and artists who treat them effectively as ends. Their attitude is a spontaneous expression of naturalism or, to give it its old name, which is its name for all time, of paganism, into which society ceaselessly tends to fall back because it has never completely left it. It is important, however, to free ourselves from it. It is impossible to place the intelligence at the service of God without respecting integrally the rights of the intelligence: otherwise it would not be the intelligence that is put at His service; but still more is it impossible to do so without respecting the rights of God: otherwise it is no longer at His service that the intelligence is placed. What has to be done in order to observe this second condition?

Here, with due apology, I am going to be obliged to play the thankless rôle of one who denounces errors, not only among his adversaries, but among his friends. To excuse such a one, it is necessary to remember that he who accuses his friends accuses himself in the first place. The ardour of his criticisms expresses above all the consciousness of the fault which he himself has committed and into which he always feels in danger of falling again. I believe, therefore, that I ought to say, first of all, that one of the gravest evils from which Catholicism suffers today is that Catholics are no longer proud enough of their faith. This lack of pride is unfortunately not incompatible with a certain satisfaction in what Catholics do or say, nor with an optimistic air more proper in a party than in a Church. What I regret is that instead of confessing in all simplicity what we owe to our Church and to our faith, instead of showing what they bring to us and what we would not have without them, we believe it good politics or good tactics, in the interests of the Church itself, to act as if, after all, we distinguish ourselves in no way from others. What is the greatest praise that many among us may hope for? The greatest that the world can give them: he is a Catholic, but he is really very nice; you would never think he was one.

Ought not the very contrary be desired? Not indeed Catholics, who would wear their faith as a feather in their hat, but Catholics who would make Catholicism so enter into their everyday lives and work that the unbelieving would come to wonder what secret force animated that work and that life, and that, having discovered it, they would say to themselves, on the contrary: he is a very good man, and now I know why: it is because he is a Catholic.

In order that we may be thus thought of, it is necessary that we ourselves believe in the efficacy of the divine work in transforming and redeeming nature. Let us believe in it, and let us say so on occasion, or at least let us not deny it when we are asked about it. That is not what we always do. If there is one principle that our doctors have transmitted to us and insistently recommended, it is that philosophy is the handmaid of theology. Not a single one of the great theologians has not said so; not one of our great popes has failed to recall it to us. And yet, it is hardly the fashion to speak of it today, even among Catholics. Men endeavour rather to show that the formula does not really mean what it appears to mean. They think it clever to present the Christian who philosophizes as a good philosopher, because he philosophizes as if he were not a Christian. In short, just as he is a very good man, he is a very good philosopher: it isn't noticeable that he is a Catholic. What would be interesting, on the contrary, would be a philosopher who, like Saint Thomas or Duns Scotus, would take the lead in the philosophical movement of his time, precisely because he was Catholic.

It seems to be thought sometimes that a philosophy which confessed itself Catholic would be discredited in advance, and that, in order to make truth accepted, the cleverest way is to present it as if it had nothing to do with Catholicism. I am afraid that that is even a tactical error. If our traditional philosophy doesn't find today the audience we would wish for it, it is not at all because it is suspected of being sustained by a faith, it is indeed rather because, being so, it pretends not to be so, and because no one wishes to take seriously a doctrine which begins by denying the most evident of its sources. Run through the history of French philosophy in these latter years; you will see that Catholic thinkers have been taken seriously by the unbelieving in the exact measure in which they have put in the first place what, for them, is really first: the person of Jesus Christ and His grace. Let a Pascal or a Malebranche be born to us tomorrow, I promise them that no one will reproach them for being Catholics, for everybody will know that their Catholicism itself is the source of their greatness. They will wonder: whence comes this greatness to them, and perhaps will desire the faith which has given it to them.

It doesn't depend on us that we be a Pascal, a Malebranche or a Maine de Baran, but we can prepare the ground which will favour the action of their successors when they do come. We can so act that it may become easy for their successors to surpass these great minds, by clearing the ground of difficulties which, avoidable in themselves, might otherwise retard their action. We shall do so only by restoring in their fullness the Christian values, that is to say, above all by fully re-establishing the primacy of theology.

Here, as before, and with perhaps even greater emphasis, I will say that the great danger consists in thinking that, for the intelligence which wishes to refer itself to God, piety dispenses with technique. One might be tempted to address the contrary reproach to those who lean in that direction, and tell them that they act as if technique took the place of piety for them, but I do not think that that is what happens. Such men have not only acquired a faultless mastery of their science or art, and are at times the admiration of their equals; they have also kept the most integral faith joined to the most lively piety. What they lack is that they do not know that, in order to link together the science they have acquired with the faith which they have preserved, a technique of faith is necessary along with that of science. What I see in them, rather let us say what we perceive fundamentally in ourselves, as an ever-present difficulty, is the inability of getting reason to guide itself by faith, because, for such a collaboration, faith no longer suffices; what is wanting is that sacred science which is the keystone of the edifice in which all the others ought to take their place: namely, theology. The most ardent theologian, animated by good intentions, we have said, will do as much harm as good, if he pretends to "utilize" the sciences without having mastered them: but the savant, the philosopher, the artist, animated by the most ardent piety, run into the worst misfortunes, if they pretend to refer their science to God without having, if not mastered, at least practiced the science of divine things. Practiced, I say, for, like the others, this science is learned only by practicing it. It alone can teach us what is the last end of nature and of intelligence, putting before our eyes these truths which God Himself has revealed to us, and which enrich with such profound perspectives those truths which science teaches. As a converse, therefore, of what I said of an apologist, I will say here that it is possible to be a savant, a philosopher and an artist without having studied theology, but it is impossible without it to become a Christian savant, philosopher or artist. Without it, we can indeed be, on the one hand Christians, and on the other hand savants, philosophers or artists, but never without it will our Christianity descend into our science, into our philosophy, into our art, to reform them from within and vivify them. For that, the best will in the world would not suffice. It is necessary to know how to do it, in order to be able to do it, and like the rest it cannot be known without being learned.

If, therefore, we owe to our Catholicism our respect for nature, for the intelligence and the technique by which the intelligence scrutinizes nature, to it also we owe the knowledge of how to direct this science towards God, Who is its Author: *Deus scientiarum dominus*. And just as I permitted myself to recommend the practice of the scientific disciplines or artistic disciplines *to those whose vocation it is to serve God in these domains,* so also I permit myself to recommend with all my power the teaching and practicing of theology to all those who, having mastered these techniques, seriously want to refer them to God.

We must not conceal from ourselves that, in the one case as in the other, it is a question here of undertaking a long effort. Nothing less will be necessary than the collaboration of all good wills qualified to succeed therein. We are here facing a new problem, which demands a new solution. In the middle ages, the sciences were the privilege of the clerics, that is to say, of those who possessed by their very state the science of theology. The problem, therefore, did not arise for them. Today, due to an evolution, the investigation of which is not within our present scope, those who know theology are not those who make science, and those who make science, even when they do not despise theology, do not see the least inconvenience in not knowing it. There could be nothing more natural on the part of those who are not Catholics, but nothing more abnormal on the part of those who make profession of Catholicism. For even if they experience the most sincere desire of putting their intelligence at the service of their faith, they will never succeed in doing so, because the science of faith is wanting to them. In order for them to succeed in that, it is necessary that they be taught, not how to make it (it is for them to find it), but what this sacred truth is, with which their intelligence longs to be inspired.

It is important, therefore, to understand that we are living in a time when theology can no longer be the privilege of some specialists devoted to its study by the religious state which they have embraced. Doubtless the clerics ought to consider it as their proper science and retain the mastery in it, for it belongs to them in full right; and not merely retain it but exercise it in all its fullness, for it is a question of life or death for the future of the Christian life, in souls as well as in society. As soon as theology surrenders the exercise of its rights, it is the word of God which gives up making itself heard, nature which turns away from grace, and paganism which reclaims the rights that it has never surrendered. But, inversely, if it be desired that the word of God make itself heard, hearers are necessary to receive it. It is necessary that those who wish to work as Christians in the great work of science, philosophy or art, themselves know how to hear His voice, and not only be instructed in His principles, but also and above all be imbued with them.

Here, less than anywhere else, it is neither the number nor the extent of the knowledges which is important; it will be sufficient to choose a very small number of fundamental principles, provided that the thought of those who receive them be impregnated with them, and that they inform it from within to the point of becoming one with it, of living in it and through it, as a grafted limb, which draws to itself all the sap from the tree in order to make it bear its fruit. To choose these principles, organize the teaching of them, give it to those She judges worthy of it, is the work of the teaching Church, not of the Church taught. But if the latter can in no case pretend to the mastery, it can at least present its demands and make known its needs. That is all I have wished to do, by demanding that the truth of faith be taught in its fullness and that the magisterial function of theology recover its full authority.

I would be nourishing the most naïve illusions, if I thought I were now setting forth popular opinions. They are not so among the unbelieving, who are going to accuse me (some have already done so) of wishing to rekindle the funeral piles of the Inquisition and entrust the control of science to the Court of Inquisition. They are not so even among certain Catholics who, knowing that such ideas lead to such retorts, do not judge it expedient, in the interests of religion itself, to expose themselves to them. To reply to them, however, it is not necessary to reopen the discussion of what were the Inquisition and the affair of Galileo. Whatever happened in former times, the official and constant doctrine of the Church is that science is free in its own domains. No one pretends that philosophy and physics can or ought to be deduced from theology; Saint Thomas even taught the exact opposite against certain of his contemporaries who were making of what we call today positive science a particular case of Revelation. To demand that science and philosophy regulate themselves under theology, is first of all to demand them to agree to recognize their limits, to be content to be a science or a philosophy, without pretending to transform themselves, as they are constantly doing, into a theology. It is also to demand them to take into consideration certain truths taught by the Church regarding the origin and the end of nature and of man, not always with the intention of transforming them into so many scientific truths and to teach them as such (for they may be objects of pure faith) but to avoid in their researches aimless strayings, which are ultimately much more prejudicial to science itself than they can be to Revelation. The greater is the authority of faith, the more those who are qualified to speak in its name ought to use prudence and wisdom before committing themselves, but the more exacting and rigorous are the scientific disciplines in the matter of proofs, the more scrupulous ought they to be in putting on an equal footing all that they teach: the observed fact, the hypothesis controlled by experience and the theory which, withdrawn from all experimental control properly so called, will be replaced tomorrow by another, although today it is imposed to all intent and purpose as a dogma. A visit to the cemetery of scientific doctrines that were irreconcilable with Revelation would take us by a great many tombs. In our own lifetime, in the name of how many doctrines, abandoned since by their very authors, have we been summoned to renounce the teaching of the Church? How many false steps from which historians and savants would have been saved, if they had listened to the voice of the Church when She warned them that they were exceeding the limits of their competence, that is to say, those of science itself? We ask them nothing else: to renounce those costly and sterile experiments, and to recognize, in this sense, the primacy of theology, is precisely to renounce them.

Thus, therefore, to restore in their fullness the theological values, to do so in such a way that they descend into the thought of the savant who calculates or who experiments, into the reason of the philosopher who meditates, into the inspiration of the artist who creates, is truly to place the intelligence at the service of Christ the King, since it is to promote the coming of His reign, by aiding nature to be born again under the fruitful action of His grace and in the light of His truth.   Such is the end, such also the means, and there is no other, for the only service that Christ demands from us is to aid Him in saving the world; but it is His word alone that saves.   In order to cooperate with Him, let us listen, therefore, first of all to His word, repeat it as does the Church and not hesitate to refer to it publicly when necessary.   It does not depend on us that it be believed, but we can do very much towards making it respected; and if it happens that those among us who are not ashamed of the Gospel fail to get others to follow them, those who are ashamed of it can be sure not even to get others to respect them.

NOTES TO CHAPTER ONE

1. I Cor., 15, 10.
2. P. Damiani, *De sancta simplic.*, cap. 8, P.L., t. 145, c. 702.
3. Imitation of Christ, I, 2.
4. Imit., I, 2, 9.
5. Ps., IV, 7.
6. *De Ordine*, II, 13; P.L., t. 32, c. 1013.
7. *De perfectmonachorum*, c. XI; P.L., t. 145, c. 306.
8. *De servo arbitrio*, ed. Weimar, t. 18, p. 640.
9. Saint Augustine, *De Civitate Dei*, lib. XXII, ch. 24. We have partially followed the translation of L. Moreau, Paris, Garnier; t. III, pp. 524-527.
10. M. Luther, *De servo arbitrio*, ed. Weimar, t. 18, pp. 634-635.
11. M. Luther, *op. cit.*, t. 18, p. 638.
12. M. Luther, *op. cit.*, t. 18, pp. 754-755.
13. M. Luther, *Propos de table*, transl. L. Sauzin, Paris, 1932, p. 477. Some rather interesting views on the proofs of the existence of God will be found a little further on (p. 481). These spontaneous reflections about Cicero do not authorize one in attributing to Luther a firm opinion in favour of natural theology, but they attest, nevertheless, a hesitation in his thought on this point. In him, the Reformer has martyred the humanist.
14. M. Luther, *op. cit.*, t. 18, p. 667.
15. M. Luther, *Propos de table*, ed. cit., pp. 121-122.
16. J. Calvin, *Institution de la religion chrétienne*, ed. J. Pannier, Paris, 1936; Argument of the present book; t. I, p. 4. Cf. p. 305.
17. J. Calvin, *op. cit.*, ch. I, ed. cit., t. I, p. 43.
18. *Op. cit.*, I, pp. 43, 46.
19. *Op. cit.*, t. I, p. 52.
20. *Op. cit.*, ch. II, t. I, p. 115.
21. J. Calvin, *op. cit.*, ch. II, t. I, pp. 118-119.
22. J. Calvin, *loc. cit.*, pp. 119-120.
23. Rom., I, 20; J. Calvin, *op. cit.*, ch. I, t. I, p. 52.
24. J. Calvin, *op. cit.*, ch. I, t. I, p. 60.
25. J. Calvin, *op. cit.*, ch. I, t. I, p. 12.
26. J. Calvin, *op. cit.*, ch. II, t. I, p. 195.
27. I Kings, II, 3.
28. Saint Thomas Aquinas, *Sum. theol.*, Ia IIae, qu. 114, art. 1, resp. et ad 1m.

NOTES TO CHAPTER TWO

1. A. Lecerf, *De la nature de la connaissance religieuse*, Paris, ed. "Je Sers", 1931, p. 24.
2. A. Lecerf, *op. cit.*, p. 27.

3. A. Lecerf, *op. cit.*, p. 34. For a statement of the problem in relation to Saint Anselm, see E. Gilson, *Le sens de l'argument de saint Anselm* in *Arch. d'hist. doctrinale et littéraire du moyen âge*, t. IX (1934), pp. 5-51. In this study will be found an examination of the interpretation of Saint Anselm by Karl Barth, which need not be repeated here.

4. A. Lecerf, *op. cit.*, p. 34.

5. A. Lecerf, *op. cit.*, p. 75.

6. II Cor., 10, 5.

7. Saint Thomas Aquinas, *Sum. theol.*, I, 1, 8, resp. et ad 2m.

8. A. Lecerf, *op. cit.*, p. 124.

9. Rom., I, 21.

10. A. Lecerf, *op. cit.*, p. 33.

11. A. Lecerf, *op. cit.*, p. 45.

12. A. Lecerf, *op. cit.*, pp. 46 and 51.

13. J. Calvin, *Institution*, ch. I, *ed. cit.*, p. 48.

14. A. Lecerf, *op. cit.*, p. 176.

15. A. Lecerf, *op. cit.*, pp. 176-177.

16. A. Lecerf, *op. cit.*, p. 177.

17. A. Lecerf, *op. cit.*, p. 161.

18. A. Lecerf, *op. cit.*, p. 52.

19. By recalling to us Rom., VIII.

20. K. Barth, *Parole de Dieu et parole humaine*, ed. "Je Sers", Paris, 1933, p. 214.

21. Without doubt Rom., VIII, 19-22.

22. K. Barth, *op. cit.*, p. 186.

23. K. Barth, *Trois Conférences*, Paris, ed. "Je Sers", 1934, pp. 29-30.

24. K. Barth, *Parole de Dieu et parole humaine*, p. 186.

25. K. Barth, *op. cit.*, p. 261.

26. K. Barth, *op. cit.*, p. 201. Cf. p. 203.

27. *Oeuvres de Calvin*, ed. "Je Sers", Paris, 1934, t. II, p. 175.

28. The difference between the Catholic position and the reformed position appears clearly in A. Lecerf's book, which has already been cited. For him: "The only legitimate point of departure in constructing a philosophy of religion, is one which consists in taking faith, understood as *a religious aptitude restored by grace*, as the organ of knowledge". (*Op. cit.*, pp. 47-48.) That seems to me excellent Calvinism. For the Catholic, grace restores not only a religious aptitude, but also a natural aptitude. A Calvinistic natural theology is therefore impossible, but a Catholic natural theology is possible, and that is why, as opposed to the Calvinist, the Catholic has a right to a "Christian philosophy" properly so called.

29. J. Calvin, *Le catéchisme*, in *Oeuvres de Calvin*, Paris, ed. "Je Sers", 1934, p. 25. Cf. *Confession de la Rochelle*, art. II, *ed. cit.*, p. 142.—*Confession des Pays-Bas*, art. II, *ed. cit.*, p. 180.

30. I intentionally omit the "plus évidemment" omitted by the revisers of Dordrecht. These revisers were prudent Calvinists.

31. J. Calvin, *Confession de la Rochelle*, art. IX, *ed. cit.*, p. 149. Calvin's editors justify this total condemnation of the intelligence and reason in divine matters by an appeal to Saint Paul, I Cor., II, 14. It suffices to compare the texts to see what there is in that. On the other hand, the *Confession of Westminster* (1647) is much more reserved: "Although the light of nature, and the works of creation and providence, do so far manifest the goodness, wisdom, and power of God, as to leave

men inexcusable; yet they are not sufficient to give that knowledge of God, and of his will, which is necessary unto salvation." (*The confession of faith*, Glasgow and London, 1859, art. I, p. 19.) Nothing in that agrees with the texts of Saint Paul or Catholic theology. As to knowing whether it is Calvinism, it is at least permissible to doubt it. The same remark applies to the beginning of the *Larger Catechism* of Westminster (approved by the Church of Scotland in 1648, q. 2, *ed. cit.*, p. 109); that is why we have not believed it necessary to take into consideration these adulterated forms of Calvinism.

NOTES TO CHAPTER THREE

1. A. Lecerf, *De la nature de la connaissance religieuse*, p. 18.

2. *Catéchisme du Diocèse et de la Province de Paris*, Paris, J. de Gigord, s.d., p. 1.

3. J. Calvin, *Cathéchisme*, xviii° section, *ed. cit.*, pp. 48-49.

4. Saint Thomas Aquinas, *Sum. theol.*, Ia IIae, q. 56, art. 3, resp. et 1m.

5. *Op. cit.*, IIa IIae, q. 2, art. 3, resp.

6. Hebr., XI, 1.

7. J. Calvin, *Cathéchisme, loc. cit.*, p. 49.

8. Saint Thomas Aquinas, *Sum. theol.*, IIa IIae, q. 4, art. 1, resp.

9. A. Lecerf, *op. cit.*, p. 31. For what follows on the fallibility of natural reason, see *ibid.*, pp. 31-32.

10. *Summa Contra Gentiles*, I, 4.

11. Cf. E. Gilson, *La philosophie de saint Bonaventure*, p. 82.

12. Job, XXXVII, 26.

13. Saint Thomas Aquinas, *De symbolo apostolorum*, in *Opuscula omnia*, Paris, Lethielleux, t. IV, p. 350. For the following formula, *op. cit.*, p. 351.

14. Saint Paul, I Cor., I, 24 and 30; commentated by Saint Thomas, *In I Sent.*, Prolog.

15. A. Lecerf, *op. cit.*, pp. 159-160. Cf. p. 272.

16. Saint Thomas Aquinas, *In I Sent.*, Prolog., q. 1, art. 1, *contra*.

17. *Conc. Vat.*, in Denzinger, *Enchir. Symbol.*, 16th ed., texts 1799, 1800, p. 479.

18. Saint Thomas Aquinas, *In Boeth. de Trinitate*, qu. III, art. 1, ad 3m, ed. Mandonnet, t. III, p. 64.

19. *Op. cit.*, Resp., p. 63.

20. *Traité élémentaire de philosophie à l'usage des classes*, edited by the Professors of the Institut Supérieur de Philosophie de l'Université de Louvain, 7th ed., Louvain, 1925; vol. II, p. 22. This text is referred to by A. Lecerf, *op. cit.*, pp. 29-30.

Although it was printed under his name, the formula which we are discussing was not written by Cardinal Mercier himself, but added to his text by one of his disciples. (See N. Balthasar, *Le chrétien peut-il croire de foi divine en l'existence de Dieu?* in *Revue néoscolastique de Philosophie*, vol. 40 (1937), pp. 67-74.) My reason for discussing these matters is that I was merely trying to analyze the teaching of Saint Thomas Aquinas. Now it is certain that, according to Saint Thomas, the existence of God does not belong essentially to the body of faith, and even that it is not an article of faith (De Veritate, qu. 14, art. 9, ad 9m). If that is what Prof. Balthasar has in mind when he writes that "divine faith" cannot bear "formally" upon the existence of God, we are in complete agreement. Yet, it is equally certain that, according to Saint Thomas, there are many objects of faith which are not articles of faith. (On the technical meaning of *articuli fidei*, see *Sum. theol.*, IIa IIae, q. 1, art. 6, Resp.) The point at issue is therefore to know whether or not it is possible, from the point of view of Saint Thomas, to believe by a supernatural act of faith that God exists. Even on this second point I fail to detect any real disagreement between what I have written and the position implied in Prof. Balthasar's criticism of it. I call "rational knowledge of the existence of God" that rational certitude of his existence which is caused in us by a metaphysical and scientific (i.e., *faciens scire*) demonstration. Now Prof. Balthasar himself says (*art. cit.*, p. 73): "No doubt, most of the Christians begin to believe that God exists before being entitled to say that they know it." My own question to Prof. Balthasar then is: Is not the belief of those Christians an act of faith? And if it is, is not their faith that very same divine faith of which Saint Thomas has said: "Ne multitudo hominum a divina cognitione remaneret vacua, provisa est ei *divinitus* via per fidem"? * But then it becomes impossible to maintain the thesis introduced by Prof. Balthasar into the text of Cardinal Mercier, that "a Catholic cannot by divine faith believe in the existence of God". Since Prof. Balthasar himself tells us that most of the Christians begin by doing it, he cannot maintain at the same time that it cannot be done. In short, Prof. Balthasar's justification of his own formula involves the very condemnation of it.

21. Saint Thomas Aquinas, *In Boeth. de Trinitate*, q. 1, art. 1, ad 4m, *ed. cit.*, pp. 64-65.

22. D. Mercier, *op. cit.*, p. 28.

23. Saint Thomas Aquinas, *De Veritate*, q. 14, art. 9, ad 9m.

24. *In III Sent.*, dist. 24, art. 3, q. 3, sol. 1, ad 1m, ed. Mandonnet, t. III, p. 774.

25. Saint Thomas Aquinas, *Cont. Gent.*, lib. I, cap. 4.

26. Saint Thomas Aquinas, *Sum. theol.*, IIa IIae, q. 2, art. 4, *Sed contra* et Resp.

27. Saint Thomas Aquinas, *In III Sent.*, dist. 24, art. 2, q. 3, sol. 2; ed. Mandonnet, t. III, p. 769. It goes without saying that if instead of considering merely the knowledge of the existence of God, which I have discussed as the most favourable case for the opposite thesis, we considered either a certain number of divine attributes taken singly, or especially the whole group of truths naturally knowable about God reduced to the state of science (and it is only there that they form a "natural theology" in the proper sense), it is still more improbable that faith can or ought to be eliminated from the effort to acquire them. I must, however, recognize that here, even among the Thomists, there is not perfect agreement. Cajetan seems to restrain the *vulnus ignorantiae* to the practical intelligence, which doubtless leads to maintaining, with J. Maritain, that morals at least cannot be adequately established without reference to theology. Billuart, on the other hand, does not seem to see (no more than I myself) on what this limitation is based. Whence his conclusion: "Homo lapsus, absque gratia speciali superaddita, non potest, saltem potentia morali, cognoscere sive collective sive divisive *omnes* veritates naturales tam speculativas quam speculativo-practicas . . . Nam inter veritates naturales sunt quaedam adeo arduae et difficiles, ut nullus hominum certam eorum cognitionem hucusque adipisci potuerit." *Summa S. Thomae* . . . , De gratia, diss. III, art. 2, m, 1. The classical Billuart is neither Baïus, nor even Bautain; but he does not admit the unreserved validity, the integral "health" of the intelligence in a nature wounded by original sin, and it will at least be granted that this attitude can make use of the texts of Saint Thomas Aquinas on the reasons justifying the revelation by God of knowable truths.

28. Saint Thomas Aquinas, *In Boeth. de Trinitate*, q. I, art. 1, Resp., *ed. cit.*, pp. 28-29. It is in this sense that Saint Thomas has always denied that a special grace

* *In Boeth. de Trin.* Lect I, Q. III, a. 1. (*Opusc. Om.*, Mandonnet ed. Vol. III. p. 63). Cf. *Sum. Theol.*, IIa IIae, q. II, a. 4, c.

is required for our knowledge of natural truths: *In II Sent.*, dist. 28, q. 1, art. 5; *ed. cit.*, t. II, pp. 731-732.—*Sum. theol.*, Ia IIae, q. 109, a. 1. It is a point on which he is in direct opposition to Saint Albert the Great, *Sent.*, P. I, dist. 2, a. 5 (Borgnet, t. 25, p. 59); and *Sum. theol.*, P. I, tr. 3, q. 15, m. 3, a. 3 (Borgnet, t. 31, pp. 110-111).

29. D. Mercier, *op. cit.*, pp. 23-24.

30. *Rev. des se. philos. et théol.*, t. 24, p. 132. A much more careful and better-balanced discussion of the problem is that of A. Motte, O.P., *Théodicée et théologie chez St. Thomas d'Aquin*, in *Rev. des sc. philos. et théol.*, t. 26 (1937), pp. 5-26.

31. *Sum. theol.*, IIa IIae, q. 2, art. 2, ad 3m.

32. *Loc. cit.*, Cfr. *Aristotle Metaph.*, IX, 9, 1051b, and Saint Thomas *in loc. Lect.* 11 (Pirotta ed. # 1909 sqq.).

33. Conc. Vat., in Denzinger, *ed. cit.*, text 1799, p. 479.

34. Saint Thomas Aquinas, *Sum. theol.*, Ia IIae, q. 85, a. 3, Resp.

35. Saint Thomas Aquinas, *Sum. theol.*, Ia IIae, q. 109, a. 2, ad 3m: "Magis est natura humana corrupta per peccatum quantum ad appetitum boni, quam quantum ad cognitionem veri." Less corrupted in this respect, our nature is nevertheless still corrupted, even for the most intellectual of our theologians.

36. *Op. cit.*, a. 2, Resp.

37. Because original sin has contaminated the will more than the other faculties; but the disorder of the will, a dissolution of the harmony in which consisted original justice, has its repercussion in the other faculties.—*Sum. theol.*, Ia IIae, q. 82, art. 1, Resp.; art. 2, ad 3m; art. 3, ad 3m.

38. Eph. IV, 17-18.

39. *Summa Contra Gentiles*, I, 4.

NOTES TO CHAPTER FOUR

1. K. Barth, *Trois conférences, ed. cit.*, p. 42.

2. E. Gilson, *L'esprit de la philosophie médiévale*, 2 vol., Paris, J. Vrin, 1932.

3. *La Philosophie chrétienne*, Cerf edition, Juvisy, 1933, p. 141.—On the other hand, it appears from the reading of this volume that, according to the final obser-vation of R. P. Chenu, the problem can be discussed only in the light of theology (p. 144), as was so excellently done by R. P. Motte in his report, pp. 76-113.

4. *Op. cit.*, p. 136.

5. Saint Thomas Aquinas, *Sum. theol.*, Ia IIae, q. 109, art. 2, Resp.

6. Saint Thomas Aquinas, *Sum. theol.*, III, q. 53, art. 2, Resp.

7. *La Philosophie chrétienne, ed. cit.*, p. 137. On "Christian wisdom", *ibid.*, p. 136.

8. *La Philosophie chrétienne, ed. cit.*, p. 138.

9. That is why the essential domain of Christian philosophy corresponds exactly to the limits of natural theology, but, accidentally, it exerts an influence on almost the whole of philosophy, if it is true that, according to the words of Saint Thomas: "fera tota philosophia ad cognitionem divinorum ordinetur". *In III Sent.*, dist. 24, art. 3, q. 3, sol. 1, 3°.

10. See the observations of P. Laberthonnière, in A. Lalande, *Vocabulaire tech-nique et critique de la philosophie*, t. III, Suppl., p. 111.

11. *La Philosophie chrétienne*, p. 138.

12. *La Philosophie chrétienne*, p. 137. This text is quoted here according to the *Erratum* added to the volume, which corrects the wording of p. 137, with which, how-ever, it remains entirely in accord.

13. See above, p. 79. Cf. F. Van Steenberghen, *La seconde journée d'études de la Société thomiste*, in *Revue Néoscolastique de Philosophie*, t. 35 (1933), p. 544: "a negative control exercised by faith on the conclusions of scientific research."

14. E. Gilson, *The Spirit of Mediaeval Philosophy*, New York, Sheed & Ward, 1936.

15. Concerning the import of this capital document, see the apposite remarks of Mgr. L. Noël, *Le Cinquantenaire de l'Encyclique "Aeterni Patris"*, in *Revue catholique des idées et des faits*, Aug. 2, 1929.

16. F. Van Steenberghen, *art. cit.*, p. 545.

17. Cf. F. Van Steenberghen, *La seconde journée d'études* . . . , p. 547, where he says that Revelation can interfere in order to "suggest ideas, estimates, possibilities, to the Christian philosopher which would never have occurred to him without revelation."

18. II Cor., X, 5.

19. Saint Thomas Aquinas, *In III Sent.*, dist. 24, art. 3, sol. 1, Resp.

20. Fr. Ehrle, S.J., *Die päpstliche Encyklika von 4. August, 1879 und die Restauration der christlichen Philosophie*, in *Stimmen aus Maria Laach*, 1880, p. 13.

21. Fr. Ehrle, *art. cit.*, p. 15.

22. Fr. Ehrle, *art. cit.*, p. 20.

23. Fr. Ehrle, *art. cit.*, p. 20.

24. I have been summoned to say how a Christian philosophy, if it is a philosophy which sets itself up within faith—as it "plainly" would be in my book—can be still autonomous. (*La philosophie chrétienne*, p. 138.) Another critic reproaches me elsewhere for replying to that with but vague assertions. That was flattering me, for I had not replied at all. Having tried to explain myself on the matter in two volumes, I had no hope of doing better in five minutes; but above all, I have proposed a definition of Christian philosophy which, whatever be its worth, is not that (*L'Esprit de la philosophie médiévale*, t. I, p. 39). I do not then deny having said what I am reported to have said, although I am not told where and I no longer recall myself. Having devoted six pages to defining and then describing what I understand by this expression, it seems to me that if anyone has the right to ask me for an account of what I have said there, I also have the right of expecting him to be willing to read it before going further. I therefore excuse myself for simply reproducing here the definition that I have already given and which still seems to me to distinguish Christian philosophy from other ones in the common species "philosophy".

25. The allocution *Singulari quadam*, 9th Dec. 1854 in Denzinger, *Enchir. Symbolorum*, 10th ed., Freiburg 1908; text 1643, p. 441.—Cf. "Nunc quando et originis labe in universos Adami posteros propagata extenuatum esse constet rationis lumen, . . . ecquis satis esse rationem ducat ad assequendam veritatem?" *Op. cit.*, text 1644, p. 442.

26. *Op. cit.*, text 1681, p. 455.

NOTES TO CHAPTER FIVE

1. 1 Epist. St. John, II, 15-17.

2. Saint Thomas Aquinas, *De regimine principum*, I, 14.

3. Pascal, ed. Brunschvicg, p. 572.

INDEX